Practical problem solving and everyday advice

TAROT

YOUR
EVERYDAY
GUIDE

Janina Renee

2000
Llewellyn Publications
St. Paul, Minnesota 55164-0383, U.S.A.

FIRST EDITION
Second Printing, 2000

Book design by Astrid Sandell
Editing and layout by Deb Gruebele
Cover art © 2000 by Linda S. Wingerter
Cover design by Anne Marie Garrison

Illustrations from the Rider-Waite Tarot Deck®, known also as the Rider Tarot and the Waite Tarot, reproduced by permisson of U.S. Games Systems, Inc., Stamford, CT 06902 USA. Copyright © 1971 by U.S. Games Systems, Inc. Further reproduction prohibited. The Rider-Waite Tarot Deck® is a registered trademark of U.S. Games Systems, Inc.

Library of Congress Cataloging-in-Publication Data
Renee, Janina, 1956–
   Tarot : your everyday guide / Janina Renee.—1st ed.
     p. cm.
   Includes bibliographical references and index.
   ISBN 1–56718–565–7
   1. Tarot I. title: At head of title: Practical problem solving and everyday advice. II. Title.
   BF1879.T2 R47 2000
   133.3'2424—dc21

                                           00–028427
                                             CIP

Llewellyn Worldwide does not participate in, endorse, or have any authority or responsibility concerning private business transactions between our authors and the public.
   All mail addressed to the author is forwarded but the publisher cannot, unless specifically instructed by the author, give out an address or phone number.

Llewellyn Publications
A Division of Llewellyn Worldwide, Ltd.
P. O. Box 64383, Dept. K565-7
St. Paul, MN 55164-0383, U.S.A.
www.llewellyn.com

 Printed in the United States of America

Also by Janina Renee

Tarot Spells
Playful Magic

I dedicate this book,
with all my love,
to my grandmother, Inge Weigert

Contents

Preface

I've been reading Tarot cards since the early seventies, and like most people who take up this subject, I first got interested in the Tarot as a way of asking questions about the future. However, like most people, I also had questions about situations where I already knew what was going to happen, but wondered what I could do about it. Of course, if I did an ordinary Tarot reading and it predicted trouble, I wanted to know if anything could be done to manage it or counteract it. Also, if a reading showed a potential for good things, I wanted to know how to help make them come true. As a result, I've been exploring ways to use the Tarot as a friendly counselor for almost as long as I've been into it.

This book, *Tarot: Your Everyday Guide*, has developed out of my relationship with the Tarot as an entity, and with the cards as personalities who have lessons they are eager to teach us. It explains ways that we can approach the Tarot for advice, and how the cards can suggest courses of action, attitudes to take, and other things we can do to help deal with some of the common questions that come up in our lives.

Tarot: Your Everyday Guide, like my other books, *Tarot Spells* and *Playful Magic*, takes a problem-oriented approach, applying the insight of Tarot archetypes to some of our more worldly concerns. Finding ways to bring magical and spiritual elements into the affairs of daily life has become something of a calling for me, because accommodating the real world has always been such a challenge. No doubt, life's demands are a major challenge for many of us. Although the world's mystical and shamanic philosophies inform us that we are spiritual beings—indeed that we are spirits—the multifarious and relentless pressures and demands of the work-a-day world can make us lose sight of our spiritual connection. Working with the Tarot is one way to maintain contact with the magical world, because each individual card reveals networks of meaning, relating our little mundane concerns to the larger pattern of our lives, and of the life of our cosmos. By consulting the Tarot as a guide who will show us ways that we can interact with our world, we weave a new level of mindfulness and intentionality into our life's pattern, and employ a form of magic to help restore us to the magical world.

The act of using Tarot cards for any reason is empowering, and it counters criticism that working with these cards produces a fatalistic outlook. I find that when I read my own cards (or have them read for me), I get very energized, regardless of whether the reading predicts good fortune or disaster. If the cards show something really good coming my way, I want to do what I can to take advantage of it. On the other hand, if bad things are predicted, I want to act quickly and expeditiously to stave them off, or at least to soften their impact. The knowledge that something bad may be coming my way just makes me all the more eager to exercise my own power, to show that I can beat it. Even if there's not much a person can do to avert certain types of problems, the opportunity to prepare ourselves mentally can make a big difference. There's a saying that goes, "If you can't change your circumstances, change your attitude." Here, too, the Tarot can offer advice, for it is often attitude that can determine whether a situation becomes an opportunity or a debacle. We can't expect to be able to change or control everything, but by using the wisdom of the Tarot to define our issues and frame our outlook, we can help the course of daily life run much more smoothly.

I hope that the information in this book will enable you to develop a more interactive relationship with the Tarot, as well as provide useful suggestions for improving your life.

Introduction

This book, *Tarot: Your Everyday Guide*, explains how to use Tarot cards to get advice. This book is not intended to teach you how to read Tarot cards in the ordinary way. Reading for advice requires a somewhat different mode of interpretation than conventional Tarot reading for prediction and other insights, so the card descriptions in this book are adapted accordingly. In an advice reading, Tarot cards are laid out and interpreted as showing a course of action. You interpret a card in terms of things you can do, and the central figure in the card usually models what ought to be done. You could say that the central figure represents you, doing whatever is suggested for the situation in question.

This book is especially concerned with practical matters, applying the Tarot's advice to common problems and situations that many people are concerned about, such as whether to say "yes" or "no" to an offer, whether or not to become involved in some cause or conflict, choosing between job and educational options, starting or sustaining relationships, moving or staying put, dealing with difficult people, and so on, through many of life's paths and choices. The advice interpretation sections in this book provide alternative suggestions, which are oriented to different types of questions, but are necessarily general, as each reader's concerns are unique to him or her and must be considered in their own context. However, the information provided here will help the intelligent reader to gain the extra insight needed to apply the Tarot cards' advice to situations in his or her own life. I must emphasize that you use your own common sense in choosing whether or not to act on the ideas suggested here, or in determining how to adapt them to your personal circumstances. Naturally, you must use your own knowledge, experience, and intuition in settling on any course of action or decision, and *Tarot: Your Everyday Guide* is not meant to serve as a substitute for your own wisdom.

Many excellent books have been written on what the Tarot is, how it works, where it may have come from, how its profound and archetypal symbols tell the story of the individual's journey through life, what the different cards' basic meanings are, what their astrological and Cabalistic associations may be, how to use them for looking into the future, how to read the cards to gain insight into your personal spiritual and psychological development, and how to apply them as tools for meditation. Therefore, I do not intend to write a long introduction rehashing all of this information that has already been so well expressed by so many other authors. There is a brief explanation of the nature and origins of Tarot in Appendix I for those wishing a little more information. I am eager to get on to the subject of this book, which is how to ask the Tarot for advice for common problems and situations, and I will assume that you, the reader, already know what a Tarot card is, that you quite likely already have a Tarot deck of your own, and that you have probably picked up this book because you want to learn some other practical uses for your Tarot cards.

In writing this book, I hope to add to our knowledge and understanding of Tarot card interpretation, generally, and to make us aware of the potential for additional dimensions of interpretation for the Tarot cards, individually. Shifting the mode of interpretation to apply it as advice can provide some new insights into a card's symbols and meanings. However, I have also made connections between cards' imagery and numerology, and their practical and psychological associations, to show something of the broader range of human situations and issues that relate to these cards. Tarot writers have barely scratched the surface of interpreting individual cards in terms of all of the human experiences their symbolism illuminates.

I think there is more that we can learn about the Minor Arcana particularly (the section of the Tarot that consists of the four suits of fourteen cards each, designated as the Pentacles, Wands, Cups, and Swords). These cards relate more to the issues of daily life, which are considered minor concerns compared with the profound archetypal meanings portrayed in the Major Arcana (the "main" body of the Tarot deck, consisting of the Fool, the Magician, the High Priestess, et al.). As I have already said, I am personally concerned with the relentlessness of the demands of daily life. These little things can wedge themselves between us and our spiritual natures unless we can reframe our attitudes and train ourselves to see and appreciate the spiritual components in daily life. Therefore, the interpretational sections tend to give equal space to most of the cards.

The information in *Tarot: Your Everyday Guide* provides ideas for integrating the Tarot cards' symbolism into life, even when we aren't specifically seeking solutions to problems, but just want to stretch the good energy of other Tarot readings, or of cards we have chosen to meditate on. Acting out the symbolism of a card that has presented itself to you completes a circuit of energy. It signals the unconscious that you are serious about seeking intuitive wisdom and are prepared to act on it. This creates a state of receptivity that makes it easier for unconscious knowledge to surface.

To Beginners

If you are new to the Tarot, you can still use *Tarot: Your Everyday Guide* to learn to do advice readings. Although prior experience with the Tarot is always helpful, you do not need any background to follow this book. The individual card interpretation sections are fairly self-explanatory, and the section called Reading and Interpreting Tarot Cards for Advice explains the other basic things to keep in mind. If you can shuffle a card deck and look at a picture, that's all the prior training you need.

I know of many people who are fascinated by the Tarot and would like to use it, but they put it off because they feel they don't have time to read books about it or take classes. Don't let this deter you: the best way to learn the Tarot is to get a deck, pose a question, shuffle the cards, pull a few cards, and look at them. It helps to get a deck that has picture illustrations for all of the cards; some decks use symbols for the Minor Arcana cards, similar to ordinary playing cards. It is said that a picture is worth a thousand words, and you'll find that you can get a fair idea of a card's meaning by analyzing its picture, as well as your response to the picture. The Tarot illustrations feature characters and symbols that will stir your thoughts, ideas, and memories because they speak to important human issues and experiences. Your intuitive guesses are apt to be as valid as any author's interpretation because all cards must ultimately be interpreted in the context of your own life situations and the meanings certain symbols have for you personally (similar to dream analysis). Of course, you will be able to fine-tune your understanding of the cards as you gain more experience and have the opportunity to compare other peoples' commentaries on them.

In the course of reading this book and learning to interpret Tarot cards to get advice from them, you will learn a lot about the individual cards. You will also learn how to apply the advice-reading technique, using your good judgment and intuition, to gain more specific information and advice to apply to your own unique situations, beyond the fairly general advice supplied here.

If you feel that you need more information on Tarot card reading and symbolism, you might wish to read some basic texts on the subject, such as *The Tarot Revealed* by Eden Gray, *The Pictorial Key to the Tarot* by Arthur Edward Waite, *Tarot for Beginners* by P. Scott Hollander, *Tarot Unveiled* by Laura G. Clarson, and *Choice Centered Tarot* by Gail Fairfield. To gain further insight into the mysteries and workings of the Tarot, some excellent sources are: *Tarot for Your Self* by Mary K. Greer, *Tarot for Every Day* by Cait Johnson, *The Tarot Handbook* by Angeles Arrien, *The Book of Tarot* by Fred Gettings, *Living the Tarot* by Amber Jayanti, and *Spiritual Tarot* by Signe E. Echols, Robert Mueller, and Sandra A. Thomson.

Decks Used in Interpretations and Illustrations

The Tarot card interpretations in *Tarot: Your Everyday Guide* usually make reference to the card illustrations and meanings used in the Waite deck, though they may also bring in relevant insights from older decks such as the Marseilles deck, or alternative deck illustrations such as those of the Thoth deck. The Waite deck is probably the most commonly used deck, and even many of the new and redesigned decks use it as a jumping-off point, so its imagery is apt to be the most familiar. (The Waite deck is also known as the Rider-Waite-Smith deck because its card designs were conceived by Arthur Edward Waite, illustrated by Pamela Colman Smith, and published by the Rider company.) These interpretations are also influenced by my own practice and experience in relating them to their numerical sequence and elemental associations. In doing your own advice readings, you don't have to use the Waite deck or any other decks to which I refer. The advice interpretations provided here are general enough to apply to most Tarot card versions. If you find some discrepancies, they will probably be minor ones, and you can use your common sense and your imagination to make adjustments or find areas of agreement.

Illustrations from various decks appear on the title page for each card. They are a good example of the myriad interpretations you can make based on the image drawn. The decks you'll see are: The Celtic Dragon, Golden Dawn, Legend: The Arthurian Tarot, The Sacred Circle, Shapeshifter, and The Witches Tarot.

Reading and Interpreting Tarot Cards for Advice

Asking the Question

"How can I find happiness?" "What can I do to improve my health?" "How can I attain greater prosperity?" "Is there something I can do to improve my relationships?" These are questions that many of us have in common. Barely a day goes by when we don't also have very specific questions relating to our individual predicaments. Some of these questions may include, "How can I help my problem child?" "Should I go back to school?" "What can I do to get a promotion?" "Should I take an early retirement?" and so on. There is no end to the types of questions we have, but fortunately, the Tarot can help us by giving some practical advice. The cards can suggest courses of action for resolving problems, dealing with issues, making changes for the better, and improving our luck.

To consult the Tarot cards for advice, you don't always need to have a pressing question on your mind. A question you can ask anytime is, "How can I improve the quality of my life?" or "What can I do to enhance the quality of this day?" These are questions that I like to pose at the end of my early morning Tarot sessions. I like to start my morning by lighting an indigo-violet-colored candle to my special god-force connection, which I identify with Fortuna and the gods and goddesses of cosmic order. Then I ask questions like, "How will my day go?" or "Is there anything I need to know today?" Then, if the readings don't bring up anything special that requires further clarification, or that prompts me to ask for advice on how to promote it or counteract it, I like to conclude with a question like, "What can I do to make this day go better?" or "What can I do to make this day special?" This practice enables me to fine-tune the quality of daily life, while helping me to learn more about the individual cards and how they can be applied as advice. Incidentally, the practice of Tarot reading itself enhances the quality of daily life because it brings a person more closely in tune with the magical world and frames one's thoughts in a way that makes them receptive to intuition.

As you read the directions for laying out and interpreting Tarot cards for advice, be aware that for the sake of simplicity, *Tarot: Your Everyday Guide* is written addressing you, the reader of this book, as the querent (i.e., the person who has approached the Tarot with a question for advice on some personal concern), the subject of the Tarot card readings, and the person who will be doing the reading and interpretation. If you are doing a Tarot advice reading on behalf of someone else, then frame your questions with that person in mind and adjust your interpretation accordingly.

Laying Out the Cards

When you wish to consult the Tarot for advice, set aside a time and an area where you can be calm and focused. You do not need to perform an elaborate ceremony, but it's always good if you can create a sense of sacred space by burning candles and incense, playing New Age music, and doing any other things that contribute to a mystical ambience. For those who do enjoy the experience of ceremony, the Appendix provides a Rite to Fortuna, the Goddess of Tarot, that you can perform before doing different types of Tarot readings, as well as before other types of divination.

When ready, clear your mind and concentrate on your question.

When formulating your question, it helps to write it down. You might want to write it down in a journal or on a nice piece of stationery. The act of writing helps you to clarify your thoughts, and it also engages additional parts of your brain, which, like any ritual actions you take, seems to bring extra power to any work of divination or magic.

As you think over your question, bear in mind that you are not asking for a prediction, but for suggestions on things you can do to deal with a situation. It is a good idea to phrase your questions as simply and directly as possible, asking one question at a time to avoid confusing the issue or the interpretation. If you are open to suggestion and just want some general advice, ask very general questions like, "What can I do to change my luck?" or "How can I improve my relationship with so-and-so?" This allows the Tarot to open to a broad range of possibilities.

As you gain experience with the Tarot, you'll notice that some questions lend themselves better to advice readings, and some are better suited for ordinary readings. Consider, for example, the subject of job hunting. If you'd like to get a certain type of job or a better job, you could approach the Tarot for advice by asking, "What can I do to help my job hunt?" or "What can I do to help further my career?" However, if you are already considering a job offer, it might be more to the point to phrase your question, "Will I be happy if I accept this job offer?" rather than "Should I accept this job offer?" (Of course, the "should" question also assumes that happiness is your objective.) You may want to experiment with asking your question both ways to get different perspectives. Don't let this confuse or worry you right now. The best approaches for questioning and reading will become more apparent with practice.

Once you have framed a question in your mind, and if you wish, on paper, shuffle and cut your Tarot deck. Tarot readers usually shuffle their cards well, turning some in the process, so that there will be a mixture of upright and reversed cards. If you prefer not to work with reversed cards, and some readers do not, then be careful not to turn the cards. It is common to cut the deck into three piles with the left hand, then restack them in reverse order. However, you can shuffle and cut your deck in any manner you prefer. Pull a card or cards from the top of the deck, and lay them before you.

The simplest method is to pull a single card and consider its suggestions. If you would prefer more clarification, you can do a three-card spread by laying out three cards in a horizontal row; this is the arrangement that I find most useful for advice readings, though it is also possible to do spreads with four, five, and more cards laid out in a row. In ordinary three-card spreads and some other spreads, there is a time line with the card or cards on the left end representing the past, but this does not apply in an advice reading where all the cards show what you can do in the here and now. In an advice reading, the central card is often the focal one, suggesting your best course of action. The two flanking cards can be interpreted as enhancing the central one, giving additional suggestions or offering ways to apply the advice of the central card. I look for the way the three cards harmonize, and indeed, I have found that these cards do tend to work as a whole. They typically interrelate by reflecting different applications of an action or sides of a situation. If you have some other layout with which you prefer to work, you may also be able to adapt it to advice reading by following the basic principles explained in these chapters.

Interpreting Tarot Cards for Advice

Now that you have laid out your cards and are ready to interpret them, you must remind yourself that advice readings involve a slightly different mode of interpretation than other types of Tarot readings. Rather than showing you what might happen or what is happening, the cards offer suggestions for things you can do, courses of action you can take, decisions you can make, and external circumstances you can set up.

Basically, you follow a card's advice by acting out the scene it portrays, applying it to your own life situation and the matter you have asked about. Do this by taking into consideration its combination of graphic illustration and symbolism, elemental association (i.e., its suit), its numerological significance, and other meanings that have been assigned to it by different traditions and systems of Tarot interpretation. This sounds like a great deal to think about, but the card sections that follow will go into these things more thoroughly, and you'll find that the basic sense of a card is fairly straightforward once you've had a little practice. This book discusses several alternative possibilities for the advice each card gives, depending on the type of questions that might be asked, so you must look to the suggestions that best apply to your question, and use your intuition and common sense to elaborate on the ways the cards' advice can be further adapted to your own situation.

As with any manual on Tarot reading, this book provides information and ideas on interpretation that are necessarily very general. It would not be possible to provide specific answers for all of the very unique questions and concerns that each reader will have. There is much more that could be said about the interpretation of each individual Tarot card, many more situations that could be applied, and many more levels of interpretation that could be gone into, but I have presented the most general and direct possibilities due to limitations of time and page space, and the need to keep things simple.

The suggestions and interpretations used in *Tarot: Your Everyday Guide* are not intended to be the final word on the subject. Nothing bad will happen if you choose not to follow a course of action suggested by this book, or by the Tarot cards in general. If, for one reason or another, you don't agree with certain interpretations or prefer not to follow the book's suggestions for certain courses of action, go with your own intuition, with whatever feels right for you. Tarot interpretation, like dream interpretation, is highly personal because, although the Tarot's symbols and archetypes represent common human issues and experiences, each person will respond to them differently. The suggestions for interpretation and action provided here are just guidelines, and are meant to help you clarify your position and consider your options. You can choose to do what this book suggests, or what the cards would otherwise seem to suggest—or not. Advice readings can show you different things you can do, but they don't rule out other alternatives. There may be many courses of action that would be suitable for dealing with a given situation, and advice that is good in theory may not always easily apply due to individual circumstances. As always, you can use this book's suggestions as a starting point, but then you have to use your own judgment and intuition to interpret the cards you draw in the context of your own experience and circumstances. If you decide not to take some action, or if you make another choice, at least working with the Tarot has given you the opportunity to weigh your options, and so to make a more considered decision.

Getting back to the method of interpretation: in this book, the Tarot cards' traditional meanings and graphics are used rather literally to suggest certain courses of action. This often involves emulating the personalities, setting up the circumstances, or acting out the situations portrayed in a card. It is often appropriate to project yourself into a card and identify with the central figure in the illustration in order to better envision ways to act out the scene that is portrayed. Some of the cards' applications are obvious and easy to interpret, especially if you take cues from the pictures: be generous like the man distributing wealth in the Six of Pentacles, or hold on to what you have, like the miserly figure in the Four of Pentacles. Even when a card has rather negative connotations, there are ways to utilize that card as advice, and you may have a situation that requires its tougher, more aggressive stance. In the case of the more abstract cards, there *are* ways we can act out the cards' more generalized, symbolic meanings, with some purpose in mind.

When you ask the Tarot a "should" question, notice whether the cards portray actions that imitate the thing you are thinking of doing, or the opposite. For example, if you asked, "Should I accept a job in another state?" cards that portray action and movement would say "yes," while cards with images of staying put would say "no."

Notice that traditional readings and advice readings can differ with respect to the querent's relationship to the images within a card's illustration. In traditional Tarot readings, we as querents often play the role of viewers who are on the outside looking in. If we do project ourselves, imaginatively, within a card, we may picture ourselves as standing before the character or scene portrayed, with the qualities of that character or scene representing a situation we are confronting. I say "tend to," because this is not always strictly true. Whether an image represents you the querent, or someone else who is important to you, or something that you are dealing with, or about to deal with, can depend on the nature and context of the questions asked. However, for the sake of consistency in the interpretive sections of this book, it is assumed that the central or dominant human figure within a card is the one that you should ordinarily identify with. In other words, in an advice reading, you would pretend that you are the central character, doing whatever she or he is doing, or would be doing, if she or he had to deal with your particular situation. This applies to both Major and Minor Arcana cards. The central figure is not likely to represent someone other than you, the querent, because an advice reading is more narrowly focused on what you should do, not what someone else should do, unless you are asking a question on another person's behalf. If, for some reason, you feel a strong connection to, or identification with, another figure in a card, then go with your intuition and use your judgment to adapt the interpretation based on the attitude or actions of that other figure.

Notice, also, that the cards in an advice reading, whether upright or reversed, are entirely neutral and have no good or bad, positive or negative associations, since they merely suggest things you can do, and not things that are going to happen to you. Therefore, there is no need to be alarmed if you draw a card that would traditionally herald bad news, such as Death, the Devil, the Tower, and various others.

Here's an example of how this neutrality of cards affects an advice reading, and also how readings for advice differ from other types of Tarot readings: If you were doing an ordinary reading, and you asked the Tarot, "What's in my future?" and one of the cards you then drew was the Five of Pentacles, a card that is traditionally associated with poverty and hardship, this would make for a dismal outlook. On the other hand, if you were to ask the Tarot for some kind of advice such as, "Should I loan my cousin the thousand dollars he's been asking for?" and you drew the Five of Pentacles, this might be interpreted as advice to act out the symbolism of the card by crying poor and turning down the loan request. Perhaps the Tarot foresees that your relative will misuse the money and not repay you. You can see that this different mode of interpretation is most noticeable in dealing with the cards traditionally viewed as negative.

Court Cards, Reversed Cards, and Gendered Cards

For consistency of interpretation, this book has also adopted guidelines regarding court cards, reversed cards, and gendered cards. Differences between traditional and advisory interpretations can be seen with the court cards (i.e., the Kings, Queens, Knights, and Pages). Whereas ordinarily these cards tend to represent a person or a matter, such as a communication that has entered or will soon enter your life, in an advice reading they tend to represent a *persona*, a mode of thinking and acting to adopt, at least temporarily, in order to deal with a situation at hand. Any one of us can have a variety of personas that we adopt during different stages of our lives and in carrying out the multiple functions of daily life, or in dealing with different types of situations that arise.

The interpretation of reversed cards has always been problematic. Tarot readers have not achieved much consensus about how to interpret reversed cards, and their interpretation is highly subjective, even when they have worked out a coherent system for dealing with reversed cards. Some authorities see reversed cards as representing the opposite of the personality type or situation represented, while others see them as signifying the weaker or more undesirable potentialities of a particular Tarot card. I have come to see reversed cards as indicating that the qualities of the card in question (both negative and positive) are present, but are somehow less accessible to the individual. A card's qualities may therefore be underdeveloped and may not receive their fullest positive expression in the outer world. In this way, reversed cards operate somewhat like retrograde planets, akin to Gail Fairfield's observation in *Choice Centered Tarot* (p. 24) that reversed cards can represent the more internalized aspects of the cards .

For the purpose of interpreting reversed cards in an advice reading, I have made a judgment call and suggest that since this particular card has appeared at all, we should still emulate the qualities it represents, but in a way that is more internalized, restrained, softened, toned down, or moderated by other cards' qualities. With court cards and other "people" cards, this suggests the possibility that the individual may identify too much with the personality of a certain card, and that he or she displays its most exaggerated characteristics. Perhaps the subject has become rigidly entrenched in the behavior patterns of this type and needs to be more flexible. One way a person can moderate a type that is coming on too strong is by developing some of the positive qualities of opposite types while retaining the more positive and adaptable qualities of the upright expression of the card. Note that reversed cards may also have some significance if they alter the way a figure is facing or pointing; this would suggest a different direction toward which to move, or a choice to favor.

Although some of the Tarot cards may be identified with different sexes (as in the High Priestess or the King of Pentacles), as interpreted in this book, they advocate certain modes of action. Therefore, their advice can be applied to both male and female querents or subjects. Men can adopt the Empress' nurturing manner to deal with a matter at hand, as surely as women can take up the Knight of Swords' aggressive stance when the situation calls for it. I wanted to discuss these cards in a way that would promote a sense of familiarity with the entity, the personality that is the card as I know it, and as many other people are likely to know it. Thus, when sections in this book describe certain cards in terms like "The Hermit . . . he . . ." or "The Queen of Wands . . . she . . . ," this is done in recognition of the fact that most popular and traditional versions of the Tarot have assigned them these sex roles. I do realize that there is some sexism inherent in the roles and personalities our society has ascribed to certain types and archetypes—yet people who exemplify these societally defined traditional types also exist, and we often have to deal with the situations to which they relate.

I thought long and hard about this problem when drafting the sections for the gendered cards. While I tried to avoid blatantly sexist interpretations, I realized that attempts to use sex-neutral descriptions would lead to some terribly convoluted and tortured language. The sense of familiarity with the card as a person or personality would also be lost. In the end, I cast my lot, for the most part, with tradition. Thus, for example, Kings tend more to represent power imposed on the outer world, while Queens relate to interpersonal and inner-world values. I leave it to the intelligent reader to decide to what extent she or he wants to go along with certain suggestions and interpretations, and how to reinterpret, adapt, and apply a card's gender associations to his or her own situation.

For those who have a problem with certain card genders, there are alternative decks out there, such as feminist decks with only female figures, or decks that assign entirely new personalities or images to certain cards. I believe that most of the content of the card advice sections in this book can be reinterpreted in these new contexts, where necessary.

Additional Guidelines for Interpretation

Before we get into the interpretations for individual cards, here are some basic things to think about when doing readings for advice. Bear in mind that these guidelines are very generalized and do not apply to all cards, readings, and contexts.

Odd-numbered cards are usually in favor of change, movement, and involvement, while even-numbered cards tend to favor making relationships, creating peace and stability, and maintaining the status quo. Odd-numbered cards, Wands, and Swords tend to suggest taking immediate action, while even-numbered cards, Cups, and Pentacles urge a slower pace, possibly holding back to give other things time to develop.

Cards in their upright position, especially those that evoke a strong positive response, tend to favor a contemplated action, saying "yes", while reversed or negative-seeming cards tend to recommend against it, answering "no."

Cards with human figures tend to advise emulating the central person pictured, while other cards tend to represent situations you can try to set up for yourself.

Cups suggest making choices in favor of relationships and of spiritual and emotional needs; Pentacles direct our attention to material concerns and security; Wands urge energetic involvement in projects and enterprises; and Swords denote a need for confrontation and struggle.

If the cards you draw don't seem to apply to your situation—for example, if you ask for advice about love, and get a bunch of cards that relate more to business matters—it may be that you have some other issues that are vying for your attention, and possibly also getting in the way of the other things you are concerned about. In that case, just read and think about the interpretations you have drawn, then ask your question again, or try again later, perhaps after a few hours have passed.

To go beyond the basic suggestions provided here and elicit more information from the cards, examine them for additional symbols that may be meaningful for you, or that can be applied to your situation in a very special way. Sometimes, some small item in a card's illustration takes on special significance relative to your question and concern, and wouldn't be so meaningful or relevant under other circumstances. For example, I once did a three-card spread as a morning reading to predict how my day would go, and two of the cards had pictures of boats in the background. As it happened, I was invited to go sailing that day, so the images of the boats took on more meaning than they normally would. After you've considered the cards' basic meanings, take a closer look at the pictures and notice whether any featured objects, such as buildings, the landscape, animals, and so on, relate to your concern and have a special message for you.

Another thing to consider when looking over the cards' illustrations is which direction different figures are facing, pointing, or riding. For example, if you are trying to choose from a number of options, and a figure within your layout points to an adjacent card, or to an item or symbol within that card, that object may represent an especially favorable action or choice to make.

You can get additional ideas from your advice readings by picturing the card as telling a story, with you as the protagonist. Perhaps you had exercises back in your school days where you were given a series of pictures and asked to make up a story about them—this method is similar. For example, suppose you have been experiencing a period of apathy and energy loss, so you ask the Tarot what you might do to revitalize yourself. One of the cards you draw is the Knight of Cups. As general advice, this may suggest that restoring energy depends on doing things that revive your libido, especially by opening to a new love relationship. To get more out of this, you can project yourself into the card and use stream of thought to tell a little story, like, "I am a knight on a quest. What am I looking for? I think that I am looking for love. Perhaps I will feel more energized if I have someone to share good times with. I notice that I am not moving very fast, and I am carefully holding a cup up before me. I do not want to spill it. I think that it contains something that tastes very good and has special powers. Can I see my reflection in it? There is a stream that I will have to cross . . ." and so on. Consider what all of these symbols mean to you as an individual. Then, suppose that your next card is the Three of Cups. This suggests a need for celebrational connection with community, but now you can elaborate on the story by describing yourself as the knight heading toward a celebration, and talking about what you think about it, and what you're going to do, and who you're going to meet when you get there. You would continue to build your story, depending on how many cards you want to draw.

There are some things you can do to learn and understand advice-reading techniques. When you have time, play around with the cards. Go through your Tarot deck and pull out cards with pictures that are suggestive of things you often do, that you have been doing, that you feel you should be doing, or that you would like to be doing. Think about them, and then arrange them in rows to show sequences of action (e.g., illustrating the sort of work and other things you do in a typical day, or showing things you would like to do over the weekend). This will give you practice in understanding the ways Tarot cards can illustrate courses of action, and if some of the cards you've played around with come up in future advice readings, you'll already have some insight into how they speak to your own lifestyle, routines, and ways of doing things.

If you want to take a crash course in advice reading—a way to get practice and learn the card meanings faster—try listening to talk radio shows with guests or hosts who give advice to people who call in with problems. Do quick three-card spreads while you listen. See what the Tarot might have to say to such people. Because you won't have a real connection to the callers, you can't expect the cards to give very accurate or meaningful messages, but you can have fun looking up the potential interpretations, and thereby familiarizing yourself with the different cards.

Sample Advice Readings

Following are three examples of Tarot reading for advice. They show how the type of interpretations supplied in this book can be applied to individual situations, and how the techniques can then be further refined to get more insight into individual meanings. These examples are based on real situations, but some details are changed to honor privacy.

1. Here is a daily reading that I did for myself while I was working on this book: this was a day that had gotten off to a bad start because I'd had a bout of insomnia the night before. I felt sluggish and had a headache. I had a long slate of things I wanted to accomplish, many that needed to be done at home, and some errands to run, one of which would require a trip to town. The cards drawn were the Four of Swords, the Page of Cups, and the Three of Cups reversed. The Four of Swords, signifying a restorative retreat, and the reversed Three of Cups, suggesting reduced contact with community, helped me decide to stay at home;

I realized that the errands and phone calls could be deferred until the next day. The central card, the Page of Cups, can relate to time spent focusing on the inner life, so I decided not to worry about other things that needed to be done, and to spend some time with the Tarot and other introspective pursuits. This is often a good thing to do anyway when you are unable to maintain your normal routine and you feel like your day has been shot. This reading made me feel more at ease because it gave me permission to relax and spend some time on personal interests. I didn't entirely heed the cards, because later I did go to town, but I was in a more relaxed frame of mind, having spent time earlier devoted to focusing on personal issues.

2. Jennifer is a woman who was owed some money by a man who had previously been conscientious in making regular payments toward the debt he owed her, but then stopped abruptly, and months passed without word from him. She wondered what to do to get him to resume payments, so she wrote him a cordial, uncritical letter, and mentioned that if he was suffering some hardship, she would be willing to receive smaller monthly payments of whatever he could afford. She still didn't hear from him, so we consulted the Tarot. First, a regular reading, done to assess his situation, indicated that he was reasonably well off and seemed to be in a position to pay her. Jennifer then asked the Tarot what she should do to recover her money, though she was of a mind that she should contact her lawyer and turn the matter over to him.

The cards that came up were the Eight of Pentacles, the Six of Wands, and the Hanged Man reversed. An overview of the reading suggested that she should get organized and get her stuff together, be commanding and persistent, and take some action, though in a patient and cautious manner. So far this made sense, but she wondered if there were some more specific things she could do to help things along. If she had drawn a card like Justice or the King of Swords, the reading would have been decisively in favor of legal action, but here things appeared to be more ambiguous. Since the Eight of Pentacles can deal with organizing things, she wondered if she should get documentation together for her lawyer. However, the cards were ones that advocate doing for yourself. I pointed out that the bent-over posture of the figure in the Eight of Pentacles was somewhat reminiscent of a person writing (though this normally represents a craftsperson). Although Jennifer thought it futile to write this person another letter, she decided to give letter writing one more try before turning to the lawyer. Fortunately, the debtor responded to the second letter, and resumed payments until the debt was paid off.

3. Andrew wanted to know how to deal with a sullen and resentful stepchild. The Tarot presented the Four of Swords, the King of Swords, and the King of Pentacles. The focal card, the King of Swords, is the card that I would normally use to denote Andrew himself in the types of Tarot readings that call for a "significator." In some conventional Tarot spreads, it is common to pick one card called the significator, whose qualities best represent the questioner, and set it out before shuffling and laying out the rest of the cards. Whenever your normal significator appears in an advice reading, it assures you that you should be yourself—and it is also reassuring that the Tarot really is speaking to you. In the context of the reading, the King of Swords advised Andrew to treat the situation seriously, and to be logical, detached, and fair-minded, but not to cater to the kid by relaxing order and discipline or otherwise going against his principles in order to win affection. However, the presence of the King of Pentacles suggested a secondary persona to act out. This was not saying that Andrew should go against his King of Swords nature, but rather that he should supplement it by focusing more on his role of provider.

Andrew decided there was more that he could do to provide a materially secure and comfortable home environment; again, he was not trying to bribe the child's affections, just putting extra money and energy into enhancing the quality of life at home. This interpretation was buttressed by the third card, the Four of Swords. In this case, Andrew related to the idea of making home a safe space where differences and opinions are honored, which is more in keeping with kingly presence than an alternative suggestion for the Four of Swords, which is the need for recuperative retreat. The Four of Swords also denoted the need to allow time to pass, accepting that the process of improving the relationship would take its own pace—and so it has, though even sooner than might be expected.

Additional Dimensions: Eliciting Advice from Other Tarot Readings

Interpreting Tarot cards in terms of the advice they can offer adds another dimension to ordinary Tarot readings and meditative practices. For example, it is a common practice to draw one Tarot card a day, whether randomly or in some sequence, to study its traditional meanings as well as its personal significance. By considering the types of actions this card might suggest, we can expand our understanding of it.

It is also possible to apply advice interpretation to Tarot readings done to see the future, or to gain information about a situation, as a way of gaining more insight into the possibilities the cards are showing you. As it is, in conventional Tarot reading, advice is often extrapolated from the cards. For example, the presence of a card like Strength shows that you will be strong, so it behooves you to continue to draw on your personal strength. On the other hand, the appearance, in a conventional reading, of a card like the Devil, which usually shows bondage to self-defeating behavior problems, suggests a need to behave in an opposite manner to counteract the card's ill omen. In the example of Strength, the advice by extrapolation in a conventional reading is similar to advice interpretations. When you get readings promising good outcomes, it makes sense to sustain your luck by doing more of the same, continuing to act out the things you've been doing right. Not all card contexts lend themselves to this sort of interpretation, but simple spreads showing present actions leading to positive future consequences can often be viewed this way.

When you get a very fortunate outcome in a Celtic Cross reading, you can reread cards seven through nine as advice to be applied. The Celtic Cross, for those who are unfamiliar, is the most popular layout in use for in-depth readings. A more thorough description of the Celtic Cross spread is provided in the Appendix. This layout can provide an overview of an important situation or show you where you're at on your life path. This spread uses ten cards, with its first six cards forming a cross that shows the nature of your situation or your mental state, what is acting at cross-purposes to you, your subconscious motivations, the past influences that inform you, your guiding objectives, and the direction your life is headed. The last four cards form an adjacent vertical bar and depict your position or persona, the environmental situation, the issues at stake, and the outcome. While the cards in the crosslike part of the spread tend to represent major forces that are acting on you, the last four cards portray conditions and attitudes that can be changed if you are willing to change your attitudes, actions, or circumstances. Therefore, if you like the last card, the outcome card, you can look back over the previous three cards and consider them as validating what you should remain mindful of and what you're doing right.

When a conventional reading predicts misfortune, you can reshuffle the cards and do a reading for advice, asking how to avoid or mitigate the undesirable outcome. However, if you want to get a little more out of the original reading, you can sometimes play around with the cards by reversing them and then pondering whether their reversed meanings can be interpreted in terms of advice. They may show how some of your behavior in the outer world might be better dealt with as an issue for inner work, or how things you are repressing or internalizing might be brought out, aired, and dealt with publicly. I caution that this technique does not always apply, and is not meaningful within many contexts. It also has a disadvantage in that it involves a closed system. Although I will sometimes use card reversal as a tool for insight, if I want more specific advice about making real changes, I do a separate advice reading. I seek advice from the extra reading because sometimes the only way to bring about change is to bring in an unexpected outside element.

Concerns about Accuracy

The longer I work with the Tarot, the more I am impressed, in fact astonished, at the information and insights the cards have provided me. However, I want to emphasize something about accuracy in Tarot readings, as applied to both readings for prediction and readings for advice. It is important to weigh and balance the information you get out of a reading with your own knowledge, experience, and common sense. Because card readings can be inaccurate, you cannot rely on the messages of the cards alone when very important decisions need to be made. I consider myself to be a pretty good Tarot reader, but I get false readings often enough. Sometimes it may be that there are external facts or conditions that I don't know about or fail to consider. Sometimes it may be that there are nuances in the cards and their messages that are beyond my ability to perceive and interpret. When predictions don't materialize, it may be that my having been forewarned caused me to alter something in my attitude, behavior, or circumstances that thereby altered the outcome—and indeed, there are cases where this is the goal of divination.

I believe that Tarot cards and other oracular objects and techniques are able to work because there is a great cosmic ordering principle that encourages objects, entities, and events in our lives to align in ways that reflect our inner and outer realities. However, I break ranks with some New Agers in that I don't believe that everything is always one hundred percent meaningful, at least not one hundred percent of the time. I believe that there are genuinely random occurrences too. To better determine whether a Tarot spread's messages are accurate and meaningful for you, ask yourself whether they make sense in relation to the question you asked, whether they complement other information you have gathered, and whether they spark an "aha," a feeling of rightness. You can then use the cards' advice to supplement, not to supplant, your own impressions and judgments.

A Word on Ethics

In case I don't always make it clear enough in the card write-ups, I want to emphasize that a Tarot card's suggestions for advivce must always be interpreted within an ethical framework. Sometimes a card may suggest dealing with a situation aggressively, sometimes passively, depending on the nature of the cards drawn in response to the questions asked. Whatever the situation, it is important that any course of action be sensibly carried out in a way that harms no one and honors your necessary obligations to other people. Also, if risks are indicated, they should be calculated risks based on rational assessment of your own means and capabilities.

The Major
Arcana

0
The
fool

Rider-Waite Tarot

Witches Tarot

Celtic Dragon Tarot

0: The fool

The Fool represents the individual in a pure, childlike state, open to learning and experience. His journey is the individual's progress through the lessons of the Tarot, which is the quest of becoming oneself. Some philosophers suggest that we come into this world as individuals with a purpose and a core self that seeks expression. Just as a crystal grows according to a certain pattern, or a cell carries the template for what it is to become, each human entity may have a pattern for unfolding. Perhaps the elements of this core self are what the Fool conceals in the pack or pouch that he carries. When the Fool comes up in an advice reading, you will be facing issues that relate to your personal program of unfoldment.

Generally, the Fool card advises trying new things, even if this means taking some chances in order to open ourselves to opportunities for growth, experience, and adventure. So put yourself in the Fool's trustful mode of being, let go of assumptions, welcome the unique and the unusual, adapt to change, maintain a state of hopeful expectancy* and a belief in serendipity, and seek out new ideas, people, and experiences. Indulge in activities that bring out your playful, inquisitive child self. The Tarot is giving you the go-ahead on new, even risky, ventures, including new projects, new relationships, and travel. Seize opportunities that come up and jump into new situations, even if you feel unprepared, like you're stepping into the void. Whatever you do, do it energetically and enthusiastically.

You may have to do some unlearning in order to get the most out of the lessons the Fool offers. As Thoreau said, "It is only when we forget our learning, do we begin to know."

If you have consulted the Tarot for help in choosing between two or more options, such as job offers, investment opportunities, or other life choices, you are advised to set out in a new direction and take a chance on the one that seems the most fun or adventurous. Such a choice will be most appropriate for your life path, and you will be magically blessed and protected.

If you have approached the Tarot for guidance with creative work, the Fool tells you that you can provoke inspiration by allowing yourself to entertain foolish

* The state of hopeful expectancy that characterizes the Fool has been described by Jean Shinoda Bolen (*The Tao of Psychology*) in this way, "If we live with a hopeful assumption that what we do with our lives is important and has meaning, and if we act accordingly with integrity, hope, courage and compassion, then 'divine intervention' provides answers when we have difficulties" (p. 81).

thoughts and do silly things. In other words, "Dare to be stupid,"† especially if you are going though a fallow period or suffering from creative block.

If you've been under some pressure, or if you seek advice on improving your health or soothing some private sorrow, invoke the healing powers of foolery, which have even been known to banish evil spirits and placate the old gods. No wonder people who read joke books and cartoons, watch funny movies and comedy acts, and look for the humor in situations are known to have fewer ailments, recover more quickly, and live longer.

If you seek the Tarot's advice because you are worried that you are too old to get involved in a new venture, take heart: the Fool is eternally going forth, and teaches us that it's never too late to start out or start over.

Because the Fool card represents an innocent and trusting young person setting out on adventure, and advises opening yourself to experience and taking chances, the reversed appearance of this card would tend to advise the opposite: say "no," or at least be very cautious about seeking new ventures, taking a trip of any sort, getting involved in relationships, and entrusting important matters to other people. Conditions are too risky at this time, and may require you to rein in your curiosity, your trust, and your exuberant spirit. Listen to that barking dog—it is the warning voice of your instinct!

† *Dare to Be Stupid* is the title of a song performed by "Wierd Al" Yankovic.

Rider-Waite Tarot

THE MAGICIAN.

I
The
Magician

Celtic Dragon Tarot

I THE MAGICIAN

Witches Tarot

I: The Magician

The Magician is a teacher who believes that every person comes into this world with a unique purpose, replete with the talents, drives, and resources to fulfill that destiny. Therefore, the Magician stimulates and inspires his students to discover and develop their potential. He wants us to recognize the magic around us, and takes joy in opening our eyes to new wonders. Communication is also part of the Magician's teaching function, related to the mercurial nature of this card. He has a show-and-tell approach to setting up karmic learning experiences, which may sometimes be tinged with the humor of the trickster.

Generally, when the Magician comes up in an advice reading, he urges you to make use of your talents, gifts, and resources, both inner and outer. The presence of this card assures you that everything you need to make magic is at your fingertips. The Magician is pictured with a number of instruments that symbolize the elemental powers of Fire, Earth, Air, and Water. In modern decks, these are usually beautiful ceremonial objects, whereas older versions of the Tarot disguised these elemental symbols as trifling things like little cups and peas in order to make the statement that most of us don't recognize the resources that are available to us. Therefore, the Magician suggests that you look more closely at what you have, because you may be overlooking important materials, options, or sources of opportunity. Here's your task: find new ways to utilize your own skills, as well as other things in the world around you.

If you are consulting the Tarot on whether to start a new project or enterprise, the Magician says, "Go for it—you have the right stuff!"

If you are wondering whether to do something about a certain situation or to hold off, the Magician suggests going forth boldly, as this is a card about taking action—whether it be to act on yourself or your environment. Remember the words of Goethe, who said, "Boldness has genius, power, and magic in it." If you are thinking about making some major life changes, now is the time to seize the opportunity.

In line with the Magician's communicative powers, if there's something special you want to bring into your life, or a change you're trying to make, *tell everyone about it*. Too often, people we already know have the power to help, or access to the resources we need, but it simply doesn't occur to us to go to our already-existing networks for help, or we're embarrassed to ask for favors.

If you wish to attract love into your life, the Magician tells you that the secret is not in *finding* the right person, but in *being* the right person. If you do the things for which you have a passion, you will project the energy and confidence that will make you attractive to the opposite sex. The same advice may apply if you are trying to hang on to a love that is cooling.

For people seeking stimulation for creative work, the Magician advises experimenting with a medium you don't normally work in, or learning more about a craft technique related to the things of nature. For example, if you normally work with watercolors, you could instead immerse yourself in learning about loom beading or rock tumbling. It may seem that these things have no relation to each other, but you will find that you will gain insights and make connections that inspire your painting, as well as other creative endeavors.

If you have come to the Tarot for advice on a job hunt, the Magician emphasizes the importance of communication. This includes putting more effort into cover letters and specific job-tailored resumes, sending a lot of resumes and applications out, and calling your personal network. Word of mouth is important here: tell everyone you know that you seek a new job; don't overlook anyone. Advertise your skills and resources, including those you may not consider applicable to a job situation. Whatever you do, don't slack off on phoning, letter writing, and pounding the pavement.

If the Magician is reversed, he generally advises you to hold off on whatever you are thinking about doing or pursuing, pull back, and conserve energy. You may be trying to do too many things and risk overreaching yourself, or it may be that certain details haven't been sufficiently accounted for or mastered yet. The Magician reversed may also be telling you that you need to go back to the drawing board, back to the basics, and work out a more realistic plan. Because this reversed card suggests that the time is not right to act on your plans, it is also good to refrain from talking about them until you have done some rethinking and reworking.

II
The High
Priestess

II: The High Priestess

The High Priestess occupies the place of knowing and invites us to look within the vast web of energies, potentials, and substance that informs both our spiritual and physical lives. This card is about subjective learning, receptivity, contemplation, and service to the Higher Powers. The High Priestess seeks an understanding of what is truly meaningful, what has personal and transpersonal value. She is particularly concerned with gaining knowledge of the Self, and understanding how that Self bridges the material environment and the invisible world.

When the High Priestess appears in an advice reading, the Tarot encourages you to try for a deeper level of understanding of whatever person, issue, or affair concerns you. To do this, you must adopt the High Priestess' mutable, shape-shifting mode of learning, which enables her to approach things from different angles, even to merge imagination into them in order to understand them. This is something with which women traditionally have more experience, since so many societies require them to submerge their individuality in service to the group. However, as with all of the Tarot cards, though feminine symbolism is used, both males and females can assume this mode voluntarily.

The High Priestess also focuses on the psychological and spiritual life, so this card advises you to do your inner work. This can include devotion, meditation, dream analysis, psychological exploration, and listening to the voice of intuition. In some cases, the High Priestess may advise you to take on some form of spiritual discipline. Because there are many spiritual paths, you must use your intuition and experience to key into the system best suited to your own needs. To help set your mind on higher things, claim a space for yourself that you can turn into a *temenos*, a sanctuary where you feel safe and undisturbed. If you are able to claim a corner of your home, however small, decorate it with meaningful objects and symbols, and do ritualistic things to enhance that sense of sacred space: burn candles and incense, and play music that puts you in a meditative mood. You can also seek places of retreat in nature.

If you have approached the Tarot about starting a new venture, getting involved in a new relationship, or making an important life choice, the High Priestess advises delay, for there is an indication that you still need to work on inner changes and growth. However, if you have consulted the Tarot for help in choosing between different life paths, such as educational or career choices, this card advises in favor of the option that permits you a richer inner life, even if there are some external disadvantages. For jobs, this card advises the sort of positions that would be more attractive to introverted people, where the atmosphere is mellow and you're allowed a high degree of autonomy. This may be especially significant if you have been forcing yourself into the extraverted, fast-paced mode that our society promotes.

When the High Priestess comes up reversed in an advice reading, it may indicate that you've been *too* preoccupied with your inner world. The Tarot may be suggesting that you turn the High Priestess' gifts of attention and insight toward your outer life and material world. This especially applies to those introverted and intuitive people who would gladly spend all of their time inside their heads. Such people, for whom relationships and attentiveness to work, physical things, and necessities, amount to an inferior function, may actually find that by getting out and around they experience more interesting insights, revelations, and synchronicities than they could in solitary contemplation. This is because a person's inferior function brings him or her in contact with the unconscious, from whence many of these magical experiences come. You may have to go back and do more of the Magician's work of exploring and skillfully managing the tangible world around you.

Rider-Waite Tarot

III
The
Empress

Sacred Circle Tarot

Legend Tarot

III: The Empress

The Empress is a complex card, for the Empress archetype possesses qualities in common with many ancient goddesses, including Hera, Demeter, and Aphrodite. Therefore, this card brings up issues related to the use of personal power, nurturing and caretaking, creativity, generativity, love, romance, and pleasure.

Because the Empress is a card of sovereignty, you are encouraged to own your own power and take a leadership role in any matter that is in question. However, as the Empress looks after the well-being of others and promotes their interests, your leadership style should include empowering other people by helping them realize their own potential.

As a nurturer, the Empress is concerned with the physical contingencies of life. Looking after life's little trivialities has always fallen to women's work, but we must not look down on or diminish the importance of this work. This card urges you to look about to see what needs, or whose needs, have to be met, and then do something about it. Step in. Take charge if necessary. Start making things happen so that you and your loved ones are properly taken care of. Extend yourself so that you are a resource to others, offering physical and spiritual nutrition. Take care of yourself and your needs as well, including the needs of your body. Learn to love and own your body so that you can be more fully present, radiating the exuberant life force the Empress represents.

The Empress card has many traditional associations with love, marriage, pregnancy, and motherhood, and in an advice reading, the Empress will always be in favor of actions and options that make and nurture relationships. In response to questions about whether to seek love, get married, or have children, the Empress unequivocally answers "yes." For a man, the Empress often represents the golden woman, the anima who embodies his idealized feminine. Although no flesh-and-blood woman can truly live up to this ideal, the cards here suggest looking for someone who in some ways embodies her—though you must be sensible about what you can realistically expect from a human woman. For a woman, on the other hand, this card advises realizing your own ideals, authentic qualities, and interests. Find ways of expressing yourself in the outside world based on the knowledge that you can best attract love by being yourself; but you must also make yourself known.

For questions on how to improve relationships, the Empress suggests bringing passion and beauty into the relationship. It's common to relate the Empress to motherly Demeter, but she also has Aphrodite's qualities, as shown by her heart sigil. However, Hera's qualities in the Empress insist that she be given equality and respect in any relationship.

If you have approached the Tarot for advice on how to raise your children, this card suggests emphasizing your loving, nurturing qualities, especially if you have been acting too critical and judgmental, or if you have been too concerned that your children meet your own emotional needs, and not the other way around. Conversely, a reversed Empress would suggest that you have been too giving, and now it's time to exercise some tough love.

If you are wondering about choosing between different job options, or generally, between different life paths, this card advises in favor of the one that allows you the greatest creative expression and gives you the opportunity to exercise the transformative power of beauty, love, and harmony.

Creativity is very important to the Empress, so this card has a bearing on creative projects. Explore your own creative visions and find ways to nurture creative energies into physical realities. This is definitely a go-ahead for any creative enterprise.

Generally, the Empress card urges you to consider all the ways, both large and small, that you can bring beauty and harmony into your environment, and to take action to improve your life and the world around you. Exercise the powers of the Empress by taking up what I call "The Rilke Challenge." In his *Letters to a Young Poet*, Rainer Maria Rilke said, "If your daily life seems poor, do not blame it; blame yourself; tell yourself that you are not poet enough to call forth its riches; because for the creator there is no poverty and no poor, indifferent place" (pp. 17–18). Although Rilke was talking about looking to everyday life for poetic inspiration, we can apply his words to serve as an inspiration for creating a poetic life. Imagine what the world would be like if all people labored to brighten, beautify, and bring good feeling into their personal spaces, as well as their local communities, instead of either wallowing in blame or pursuing the ancient blood feuds that so much of the world's population is so energetically devoted to.

One characteristic of the Empress is that she's always available to meet the needs of other people, so when this card comes up reversed in an advice reading, the Tarot may be suggesting that you direct some of that loving, nurturing energy toward yourself. Consider withdrawing somewhat from your busy activities and social connections to do some of the High Priestess' work of meditation and study. Stop being a pleaser; don't worry about trying to be every thing to every body. Indeed, the appearance of the Empress card reversed may suggest that you have been something of a codependent, and it is time to stop being someone else's enabler.

IV
The
Emperor

IV: The Emperor

The Emperor is a card about coming into your own power. When you draw this card in an advice reading, you are urged to take charge of the situation at hand. The implication is that you are facing a problem that you alone must take responsibility for, though you can bring in competent people to help. Deal with the situation by thinking big, making long-term plans and commitments, establishing order, creating structure, and providing for the well-being of all involved.

In suggesting that you carry out the Emperor card's advice about taking charge of a situation, I want to make it clear that I'm not talking about muscling other people out of the way or dominating them like a dictator. Rather, the ethical Emperor finds a niche where leadership and know-how are needed, assumes personal responsibility, performs the job with skill and competence, provides others with direction and structure where necessary, and gives credit to others when credit is due. The Emperor's ability to recognize and reward the qualities and accomplishments of other people relates to one of the prime functions of the King archetype, as described by Moore and Gillette in their study of mature masculine psychology, *King/Warrior/Magician/Lover*. They say that by giving recognition, the King gives blessing, which is "a psychological, or spiritual event" that "heals and makes whole" (p. 61). In the same spirit, we should help other people by promoting their interests wherever possible.

Generally, this card suggests that in all of your relationships and dealings with people (family, work, civic, etc.) you should assume a responsible role while at the same time providing the security and structured challenges that enable people to discover and use their own power. If you have approached the Tarot with questions about your career and other life choices, the Emperor card indicates that you should choose in favor of options that enable you to reach out for more and that give you greater responsibility, authority, and worldly position. Like the Empress, the Emperor is a card about family responsibilities. Therefore, if you are considering parenthood, marriage, or related commitments, this card suggests that this is indeed a good time to take them on, and urges you to provide a secure and loving, but structured, environment.

To fully emulate the qualities of the Emperor, it is helpful to understand the values of the previous cards—the Empress, the High Priestess, and the Magician. The Emperor card has a lot to do with the reality principle, owing to knowledge of the physical world gained through the Magician. If he has integrated the lessons of the High Priestess, the Emperor also has vision. His own vision reconciles the ability to see things both as they are and as they should be. He knows what's doable, and the best way to get it done. From there, the Emperor uses the creative qualities nurtured in the Empress to secure foundations in the physical world. If he has learned the lessons of the Empress, he'll build his structures in ways that accommodate peoples' physical and psychological needs, rather than trying to force them into modes that ignore and even hurt the body and psyche.

The Emperor is a person who likes to control the symbolic world that he holds in his hand. However, there are times when it is necessary to maintain responsibility while letting go of some control. If the Emperor comes up reversed, you may be advised to give other people—whether they be your employees, children, or others under your supervision—a chance to exercise their own power, even if this means they will make some mistakes and incur a few losses along the way. Don't try to micromanage everything. Exhort others to achieve their capacity potential, push them to achieve more than they think they can, show them the line of discipline they'll need to achieve that, and then give them the permission and power to make their own decisions.

The theme of the reversed card, that of loosening control, can also apply to the need to delegate authority or to honor the authority of others. Consider the example of certain tribal societies where there is no centralized authority or head chief. Rather, there may be a chief who leads the hunt, a chief who provides civic and political leadership, a war chief, and so on. In such societies, people acknowledge that different people can excel in different areas of leadership. Think about how this may apply to your own situation. There is no loss of honor or power in deferring to the person best suited to deal with the matter at hand.

Rider-Waite Tarot

V
The
Hierophant

Celtic Dragon Tarot

Sacred Circle Tarot

V: The Hierophant

The Hierophant is about mentoring: knowing how to apply inner wisdom and sharing it with others. It can represent the kind of teaching that helps people, makes a difference in the world, and communicates the things of value. When the qualities of this card are positively expressed, the Hierophant strengthens the social infrastructure through the transmission of meaningful forms, rituals, philosophy, and traditions.

As a card of advice, the Hierophant suggests that you deal with a situation in question by assessing your philosophical, religious, and ideological traditions and values. Evaluate these beliefs to determine which are truly meaningful and helpful. Find ways to integrate meaningful traditions and values into a coherent system that will serve you as an ethical framework, and apply it to your life by acting consistently within this framework. When you're dealing with the Hierophant card, take your issues up to a higher level. Even advice about rather mundane concerns suggests action that relates to your broader ethical and philosophical system. To model the Hierophant, think about yourself at your best—as a caring, high-minded person. If you have been contemplating any action that is not consistent with the highest standards of honor and ethics, don't do it.

Due to its connection with institutions that promote values and traditions, the Hierophant card is often connected with organized religions and teaching institutions. Thus, if you're dealing with a problem, you may be advised to seek guidance or look to the resources of religious organizations or teaching institutions. If you have approached the Tarot with concerns about career decisions and other life choices, the Hierophant may advise aligning yourself with such institutions in one way or another. Bear in mind that you can choose the institutions whose traditions you wish to embrace. If you have questions about relationships, this card may advise validating special relationships through formal and ritual commitments.

The act of teaching, mentoring, and sharing knowledge is also an important function of the Hierophant. You can emulate the Hierophant by passing useful values and traditions on to those who need or desire such structures. Also, in line with the Hierophant's concern for tradition, find ways to invoke customs or design new systems that create bonds between family, community, and others and provide a sense of continuity with the past; use these vehicles for transmitting teachings and values.

If the Hierophant comes up reversed in an advice reading, the Tarot may be telling you that your thoughts and actions may be the expression of a system of ethics, values, and traditions that is somehow inconsistent, unrealistic, or inappropriate. Question the ways in which your personal code has been shaped by parents, society, and other outside forces. Do their values square with what you envision to be the most conscientious and compassionate standard that a person could live up to? Or have they imposed inflexible rules and prejudices that do injury to your psyche and soul, or to the lives or feelings of other people? Reevaluate your personal beliefs and formulate a personal standard of ethics that engages both your feeling and your thinking natures.

VI
The
Lovers

VI: The Lovers

The Lovers is always a very welcome card because it conjures dreams of love and romance. However, this is a complex card that speaks to a spectrum of human issues in its two major themes: the need to make relationship and the need to make choices.

The Lovers card expresses the principle of eros, the drive for completeness, which is the desire to come together in union with the Other. In the highest spiritual sense, eros expresses itself in our desire to reunite with God, with the spirit of the cosmos, with the soul of Nature. In a broad philosophical sense, we desire to embrace all of our fellow humanity, while in the psychological sense, we seek to integrate into wholeness our anima or animus, our solar and lunar natures, aspects of our shadow natures, and other dualities and fragments of the Self. In the physical sense, we experience romantic and erotic love for another person—although union with that person interrelates with our desire for union with the spiritual and psychological aspects of the Other. Of course, in most Tarot readings, whether for advice or otherwise, the Lovers is most likely to denote our need for physical love and relationship, since this is a concern that is uppermost on so many minds.

When the Lovers comes up in an advice reading, it most likely recommends the making and preserving of a meaningful relationship—especially a love relationship. If you are trying to decide whether to become involved with someone, then clearly this card is telling you to do so. If there is no special person in your life at this time, this card would urge you to do the things necessary to open yourself to the possibility of finding love, which may include changing your routines, going places where you can meet people, being prepared to take chances and make sacrifices, and (sometimes hardest of all) reaching out and making it known that you are interested. Know that in making relationship, you are doing the work of the archetypal Great Goddess. According to Sibylle Birkhauser-Oeri in *The Mother: Archetypal Image in Fairy Tales*, "... in her life-enhancing aspect the nature mother is also the principle of love in its deepest sense. . . . The mother appears to seek out those who are capable of real relationship. She seems to be aware that she is unable to complete her best work, bringing wholeness, without them" (p. 134).

The focused eros represented by the Lovers card can relate to the human desire to be "the one and only" in a relationship. This longing was expressed by the modernist poet W. H. Auden, who said,

> The error bred in the bone
> Of each woman and each man

Craves what it cannot have,
Not universal love,
But to be loved alone (p. 88).

Anne Morrow Lindbergh responds to Auden, pointing out that while a "permanent, pure relationship" is not possible, or even desirable, as a continuous state, couples can nevertheless experience moments in a relationship when they are totally focused on one another. In *Gift from the Sea*, she suggests that lovers can capture the state of "together-aloneness" by setting aside time when they can experience "one-and-only moments," free of distraction (pp. 72–73). If you are already in a relationship and you draw the Lovers in an advice reading, the Tarot may here be suggesting that you bring new vitality into your relationship by doing and saying the kinds of things that enable your partner to experience these moments of being your one and only.

Some older versions of the Lovers card show a man in the difficult position of choosing between two women: a fair and innocent girl, and a darksome older woman. As applied to individuals and emotions, this may denote a love triangle. In our modern society, the third person in the triangle may not be an actual person, but an imagined Other—the "something better" that people who are unwilling to commit to a relationship are hoping will come along. If you are in a relationship but withholding commitment in the hope of finding someone more beautiful, or more wealthy, or generally more perfect, the Tarot may be handing you an ultimatum: you must choose. In its positive expression, it would normally advise you to give up the wished-for Other and value the love you have. On the other hand, there are many people who stay in abusive relationships because they fear that no one else will have them, and that they'll end up alone for life. No one should ever stay in a relationship where abuse, adultery, or addiction are involved. The reversed Lovers card may advise leaving a relationship for these reasons, or perhaps because the individuals involved are ill matched. The Tarot may foresee that someone better really will be coming along.

The Lovers card may also urge you to choose relationship at the risk of loss. Relationships do present unpredictable risks. If we put our time and energy into our business or career, we can usually expect that certain rewards will accumulate over time, whereas the long-term success of any romantic affair is highly unpredictable. Relationships also threaten our economic security because the commitment required of any romantic relationship—indeed, any kind of a relationship at all—involves the diversion of energy from other personal goals and interests. Therefore, many of us who claim to be looking for love will end up choosing business, career, or personal finances over relationships and romance. The Tarot often addresses this problem when it gives seemingly irrelevant responses to questions about love. The Lovers card puts relationship as its highest value, and reminds us of the words of Tennyson, "Tis better to have loved and lost, than never to have loved at all."

If you have not approached the Tarot about romance, but rather with concerns about career or other major life moves, then the Lovers pertains more generally to the need to make choices, related to those older versions of the card that show the man trying to decide between two women. In keeping with the eros nature of this card, you would be advised to choose whichever option best favors the making and nurturing of human relationships. To get a better idea of the nature of the choices you should make, look to the cards surrounding the Lovers. If you have drawn it from the deck as a single card, reshuffle your pack, then locate the Lovers within it, plus the card to either side of it, and study those flanking cards. Be aware that to make a choice is to make a decision, and to make a decision is an act of power. When you make a decision, even if you are fearful or uncertain whether it is the right decision, there is movement in the unconscious and movement in heaven; paths roll out before you, and the Wheel of Fortune starts spinning.

The reversed occurrence of the Lovers also denotes a need to make a decision or seek relationship, but advises being cautious, taking your time, and looking beyond appearances. In some cases, the reversed Lovers may suggest that you reevaluate, perhaps even change your mind, about some decision, relationship, or other thing to which you are thinking about committing.

VII
The
Chariot

VII   THE CHARIOT

7 THE CHARIOT

BATTLE
of MOUNT BADON

VII: The Chariot

The Chariot card portrays a rider controlling the currents of energy and emotion that carry him forward to his destiny. The sphinxes (horses in the older versions) have been described as representing the emotions, the animal drives, and the other powerful but opposing inner forces with which each individual comes to terms. The charioteer is said to represent the ego, the intellect, or the idealized Self. Some versions of this card show the sphinxes or horses pulling in opposite directions, illustrating the tension inherent in the human condition and the challenges that must be mastered by anyone who hopes to achieve anything. The Chariot's divinatory meanings usually apply to the ability to exercise will power, to move in the direction of your goals, and to do the spiritual work necessary to ensure that your inner being is in harmony with your outer purposes. These qualities are readily translated into advice, as things for which to strive.

In many advice readings, the Chariot card is especially likely to call for self-direction and self-control. Self-direction requires that you work for long-term goals and delayed rewards, and self-control requires you to suppress some of your most basic drives on those occasions when they threaten to sabotage your future happiness and security. The Chariot may also raise issues as to whom is in control. If people, forces, or other things are making demands on you, acting at cross-purposes with each other and pulling you in too many directions, you may have to try reengineering your situation, however you can, to make it more manageable. Cut back on some of the obligations and distractions in your life so that you don't have so many things competing for your attention.

In its concern for movement and direction, the Chariot can indicate a certain urgency in moving toward life's greater destinations and purposes. Thus, when the Chariot comes up, you might ask yourself, "What is the fastest and most direct route to achieving my personal mission?" and "What is the best vehicle for getting me there?" Perhaps you've been trying to reach your goals by too slow or circuitous a route, and now is the time to harness all your energies to carry you more speedily along your way. This card's active nature may also advise involvement in a new situation.

You can utilize the energies of the Chariot when you need to take decisive steps to bring about change in your life. There are certain actions we can take that, once set in motion, build momentum to carry us onward and forward, as if riding a train or rafting down a river. Some common examples would be enrolling in a particular course of study, changing jobs or signing up with a temporary employment agency, starting a small business, or joining some club, organization, or cause that enables you to interact with a broader community. If you are at all competent, and conscientious about sticking with the discipline or organization, *things will start happening* in your life because you will learn new skills, go new places, and meet new people. This is how opportunities arise and new paths of possibility open up before us. For many of us, the hard part is overcoming the doubt, distraction, and inertia that can prevent us from taking the necessary steps to get involved with something new and different—or even to get involved with anything at all.

There are some circumstances in which the Chariot can take on a special meaning relevant to modern living; it may represent an automobile. Cars and the Chariot both symbolize the way we get around in life. If you are wondering whether to get a car, or a new car, this card says "yes." The Chariot sometimes also denotes travel, and would advise you to take a trip or prepare to go some distance in order to achieve your purpose.

When the Chariot card comes up reversed, it can have different meanings related to the issues of control and direction. In some cases, the reversed card advises that you are trying too hard and need to relax control. Consider the advantages of going with the flow, letting life happen to you. The Chariot reversed can also represent the act of retreating or backing up, so this card may suggest changing directions and going back the way you came. Alternately, this reversed card may urge you to get off of, or out of, whichever vehicle you are riding into the future because the energy may be carrying you in a direction you don't want to be going.

Rider-Waite Tarot

VIII
Strength

Witches Tarot

Legend Tarot

VIII: Strength

The Strength card reveals the great power each of us may access. Its conventional depiction of a woman taming a lion indicates that a key to inner strength is the ability to tame the animal nature. However, the woman may also be identified with her companion lion through this card's symbolic correspondence to the sign of Leo, which suggests ways that we may align with the animal powers to achieve greater success and personal harmony.

As a card of advice, Strength's applications are broad and general, calling for stamina as well as strength of character. You may have to muster all of your energy in one big push to get something accomplished, or you may have to assert your own rights and interests in some matter in question. You are dealing with situations that require a show of presence, and possibly also a show of force. Exercise your strength by projecting yourself. As Walt Whitman says in *The Song of the Open Road*, "We convince by our presence." This is a matter where everything rests on your determination, and perseverance is needed to carry things through.

For dealing with unpleasant situations, this card tells you that it's time to tackle your problems, to gather courage, and confront obstacles and fears. However, when dealing with difficult people, Strength's graphical depiction and traditional interpretations suggest that the best way to do this is gently, considerately, with finesse, and with respect for the well-being of others. Some old adages that come to mind are, "You can catch more flies with honey than with vinegar," and "Walk softly, but carry a big stick."

Regarding questions about relationships with others, Strength suggests that you need to be the strong one, to be there to help and support loved ones, coworkers, and others.

The Strength card also has a lot to say about matters of self-improvement: strive for strength of body, mind, and spirit. The physical nature of this card is evident, so you are especially encouraged to look to the needs of your body, to assure your health and vitality. Get into a program of exercise, diet, and nutrition; of course, this will require that you make personal development a priority. Also, explore alternative therapies and philosophies that are concerned with building the life force, and find ways to boost this flow of energy through your body and your life.

Writers and interpreters of the Tarot have often commented on how this card's portrayal of a woman handling or taming a lion denotes a need to overcome our animal nature. For people whose physical drives are out of control, as in the case of various addictions and destructive behaviors, the Strength card obviously urges getting a handle on these problems. However, due to the conditions of life in a mechanistic world, there are many people for whom a quite different problem applies, and in their case, the Strength card may suggest a need to get in touch with the animal nature. This animal nature can relate to the *criatura* or "wild nature" that Clara Pinkola Estes speaks of throughout her book, *Women Who Run with the Wolves*. Estes makes a connection between the strong woman and the wildish nature, stating, "A healthy woman is much like a wolf: robust, chock-full, strong life force, life-giving, territorially aware, inventive, loyal, roving" (p. 12). Of course, these same qualities apply to men, and other versions of the Tarot have used a male figure for Strength. By getting closer to the instinctual Self, we can draw on libidinal energies that can fuel us, giving good health and joy in life, and enabling us to persevere against obstacles. This is one reason why this card has been renamed "Lust" in the Thoth deck. Angeles Arrien analyzes the universal symbolism of the Thoth deck in her *Tarot Handbook* and relates "lust" to "lustre," stating that, "People who exhibit strength also exhibit an inherent lustre or radiance" (p. 66).

When you draw the Strength card reversed, the Tarot favors firm but soft approaches to your problems. When you have confidence in your own powers, you can afford to speak more softly, to go easier on people. Don't come on too strong and pull your punches. Be secure enough in your own strength to show vulnerability. This means being more trusting, letting go of psychological body armor and other defensive stances, and being willing to bend. This particularly applies to concerns about relationships and other dealings with people, and it also suggests trusting the process of the universe. Since Strength is a card of presence, the reversed card may also indicate a need to maintain an interest in a matter or conflict in question, but back off somewhat—your full involvement is not appropriate at this time.

IX
The
Hermit

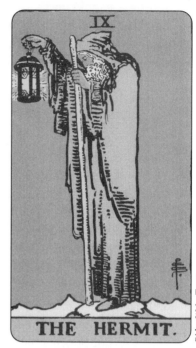

Rider-Waite Tarot

Golden Dawn Tarot

Celtic Dragon Tarot

IX: The Hermit

The Hermit embodies the archetype of the wise elder, the inner sage who can help you along your life path, and can be called upon for illumination and guidance.

It helps to think of the hermit figure of folklore, who is both a seeker of wisdom as well as one capable of dispensing knowledge to others. Although the Hermit traditionally retreats into wilderness for solitude, he also serves as a guide to lost wanderers who happen upon his secluded cabin and pilgrims who seek him out. Versions of the Tarot that show him with a burden on his back, cautiously making his way along with a walking stick, remind us that the Hermit must deal with the same cares and limitations as everyone else. This teaches us that all fellow humans are potentially our teachers, that each individual has light and wisdom to share, and that some of our most meaningful lessons come from those individuals from whom we least expect it. In fact, the Hermit's favorite teaching style could be the Socratic method, posing questions that help students access their own inner teachers.

When the Hermit comes up in an advice reading, there are many levels of interpretation that you can consider. You must use your intuition to settle on the most suitable interpretation, or find a way to harmonize these levels of potential meaning.

First, consider the graphic representation. If this card is part of a larger spread, to which card, or pictorial element within a card, does the Hermit's lamp point? It may be that the image adjacent to the lamp is emphasized as your best course of action. If the card is reversed, see what image the lamp points to here—this may be a case where the graphic relationships between the cards are more significant than the usual reversed meaning. Also, does the lamp (normal or reversed) point to the left or the right? The direction the Hermit is facing may differ in different Tarot decks, though most commonly, he faces left. If the Hermit faces to the left, this may also advise a need to look into unconscious sources of wisdom.

Because our culture tends to regard the left as relating to the past and the right as the future, the Hermit may also indicate that the answers you seek lie in the one direction or the other. If the Hermit directs you to look into the past, some backtracking may be necessary. No matter how well a person may be advancing in his or her unfolding development, there can come a time when it becomes necessary to pause, turn around, and gaze backward. At such times, we feel compelled to consider which facets of ourselves, which of the things we have valued, were either forcibly or voluntarily left behind on the roads our life has taken. This is a time to reassess and rediscover the things that have been left behind, because some of these may be the very things that could give you newfound inspiration and joy. If you wish to attract love or better relationships, this may advise rekindling relationships with past acquaintances. In looking to the past for answers to self-fulfillment, you might also try to recall what you were like and what you were doing at age nine. Nine is the Hermit's number in the Tarot sequence, and it has also been found that around age nine, children are really coming into themselves, energetically exploring their interests and expressing their personal uniqueness. Unfortunately, after this age we succumb to increasing pressures to conform and meet the expectations of others. Memories of who you were and what you enjoyed at that age can shed light to set you back on your life path if you feel that you have strayed. This advice may especially apply if you have consulted the Tarot for creative inspiration, or if you are considering a career change or some other major life choice.

If graphic interpretations don't seem to apply, then the Hermit may relate to the principle of seeking, generally. The Tarot is hinting that there is some wisdom or some piece of information out there that needs to be found and integrated. It would be well to seek a better understanding of the situation in question before taking further action. The Hermit may also suggest seeking a mentor who embodies the qualities of the wise elder archetype for an opinion on how to proceed with the matter in question.

This card may also advise you to model the Hermit's life of contemplation, solitude, and service to Deity, as well as service to those who seek your help and counsel. It suggests that you have reached a point in your life where the turning within is appropriate and also deserved (many of us feel that we don't have a right to claim time for ourselves). Also, from your own position of wisdom and maturity, you should be tolerant of other peoples' inexperience, and be willing to offer your advice and assistance to them.

Some of the other symbolism in the Hermit card may apply to requests for advice. In keeping with the mountain symbolism that is often featured in the Hermit card, take the high ground, especially if you are faced with making a choice or are involved in an ethical dilemma.

If the Hermit comes up reversed, and the graphic interpretations don't seem to apply, it may indicate that you have been looking too hard for something or in some direction, and that now is the time to let it go. Perhaps your search efforts have been yielding diminishing returns, or you may even have wandered into a blind alley. Perhaps you are one of those people who doesn't like to act on a matter until you can gather as much information as possible, which can result in putting action off indefinitely. This reversed card suggests that the time for reflection and information gathering is over, and the time for action—or at least a decision—has come.

X
The Wheel
of fortune

X: The Wheel of Fortune

In the Wheel of Fortune card, we meet the goddess presence behind the Tarot itself. Fortuna was a goddess of fortunetelling, among many other things, and she had some famous oracles. At Praeneste, the most popular oracle in old Italy, people sought her advice by drawing wooden tablets from a chest. These tablets were inscribed with messages, though their meanings were often mysterious, and the individual had to figure out how the message applied to his or her own concerns. As a goddess of luck, chance, and cycles of change, Fortuna also presided over the mutability of human fortunes—and every person was thought to have an individual Fortuna, similar to a guardian angel. Changes in fortune were seen as part of a natural process, like the cycle of the seasons. Fortune's Wheel, the Rota Fortuna, was a very common image in medieval and renaissance art, though in earlier times Fortuna was usually pictured holding the cornucopia, the symbol of the abundance that she brings forth.

Folklore describes the lucky person as "Fortune's child" or "sitting in Fortune's lap," or even as "Fortune's playmate," so you can see that the goddess presence associated with this card is one who will take you under her wing and take care of you. As a teacher, the Wheel of Fortune card urges us to be aware of life's processes, to see how the inner wheels turn, to appreciate the laws of cause and effect, and to recognize our own place in the cycles of change.

When the Wheel comes up in an advice reading, your question may relate to a situation that is part of a regular cycle, a cycle that is part of your own personal pattern; however, you may be at a new or pivotal point in this cycle. You should ask yourself what has brought you to this place: how have your own actions brought you to this place, and where do you want to go from here? Be alert to new possibilities. With boldness, decisive action, and creative thought, you can change your fate by turning the Wheel of Fortune. To effect some change, start now by laying the groundwork; do what you need to do to get the process going. The process will carry you forward and things will work out for you.

This card also reminds you that things change, so it is wise to live in a manner that is accommodating of change. Rigidity and resistance to change often lead to a harder fall. Practice adaptability, versatility, and humor, because there are some life changes over which we have very little control.

As an advice card for people concerned about enterprise, advancement, and prosperity, it helps to remember that Fortuna is identified with the planetary principle of Jupiter, which is about being expansive and magnanimous. In myth, Fortuna was sometimes represented as Jupiter's mother, and sometimes as his firstborn child. Therefore, this card tells you that the time is right to reach out for more, even if you have to extend yourself somewhat or take on a challenge or risk. If you were raised to believe that you do not deserve to have more—turn this attitude around by going for the biggest and best, with the blessings of Jupiter Optimus Maximus. Think of yourself as "Fortune's child" and adopt an attitude of entitlement.

If you have consulted the Tarot because you are thinking about making an investment, getting involved in a new relationship, or trying something new, but are concerned about the risk, this card suggests that you take a chance and spin the wheel. If this comes up in regard to a decision as to whether to make a change or to leave things as they are, it indicates that you should go with the change.

If your question relates to a problem that has its roots in the past, the Wheel of Fortune assures you that you can come back to the places where you've been before, but as a changed person with a new outlook and deeper understanding. Use this awareness to rectify old mistakes and make up for missed opportunities.

The spokes on Fortune's wheel represent the polarities and states of opposition that Fortune sometimes casts us into—situations in which we find ourselves doing the opposite of what we want, or what we would normally be inclined to do. The astrologically minded will think of the polarities of the horoscope chart: Self versus Other, home versus career, and so on. From this perspective, being on the down side need not be perceived as such a terrible thing, for reversals force us to experience opposite states.

If the reversed Wheel of Fortune appears in an advice reading, this card suggests that you should seek a change of state that will allow you to learn lessons and gain competence in areas of life you would otherwise avoid or neglect. For example, if you have been active in the outside world, you might think about exploring the inner life, or if you have been content to stay close to home, find pleasant ways to get out into the world, into the thick of things.

XI
Justice

X JUSTICE

XI: Justice

In the Justice card, we meet a goddess presence who represents truth, fair-mindedness, and personal integrity. She has been personified as Dike, Astraea, Themis, Isis, Libera, Urania, Maat, Nemesis, and by many other names and aspects. Justice was often counted as part of a triad, along with Eunomia (Wise Legislation) and Eirine (Peace). Alexander Murray's *Who's Who in Mythology* states that because of her "profound wisdom and open truthfulness" she acted as counselor to the gods (p. 128). In *Sophia: Goddess of Wisdom*, by Caitlin Matthews, the nature of this goddess is expressed in the aretology of Isis, who claims:

> I gave and ordained laws for men,
> which no one is able to change . . .
> I made strong the right . . .
> I made the right to be stronger
> than gold and silver.
> I ordained that the true should be
> thought good . . . (p. 66)

The ancients believed that when truth and justice prevail on earth, the harmony of the cosmic order is maintained. Thus, as Moera, this goddess was concerned with the role of reason and right action in social affairs; as Maat, she upheld truthfulness and right order; and as Themis, she was concerned with the operation of divine will and natural law, as well as hospitality and ritual relationships within human society. The currently popular plea, "If you want peace, work for justice," reflects the interests of these goddesses in upholding the world order.

In an advice reading, the Justice card is broad and general in its applications: in whatever situation you're dealing with, protect your personal integrity as well as your rights, be objective and fair minded, balance your own needs with those of others, and *do the right thing*. When we act justly toward others, we are doing the work of the goddess.

If you have consulted the Tarot about an issue involving your personal rights, Justice advises standing up for them. The Tarot reminds you that you are not defenseless—you have a sword (your mind), so use it sharply and effectively. This card also suggests invoking legal authorities, and the implication is that they will be favorable to your case. However, the Justice card also urges us to honor agreements and responsibilities, even those we'd like to back out of. Sometimes we inadvertently make bad bargains, but we have to honor them anyway because a deal is a deal.

In upholding the goddess' concern with honesty, you may have to become a truth speaker, saying the things that need to be said, perhaps saying things that others would prefer not to hear. Tell the truth and let the chips fall where they may.

If conflicts arise, listen carefully to the arguments of all parties involved, maintain an emotionally detached manner, and weigh the alternatives carefully. Also, in keeping with the symbolism of equilibrium, balance, adjustment, negotiation, and relationship with the Other, when the Justice card comes up in an advice reading you may need to make some compromises, and even sacrifices, in order to achieve a harmonious balance between your own needs and desires, and those of others—including the requirements of society. It will be easier for you to negotiate your right relationships with others if you have clearly defined personal boundaries, so that you know what you're willing to give up or put up with, and what rights and principles you will stand firm on.

Justice also relates to principles of adjustment, and the adjustment periods we often undergo in new situations, affairs, working relationships, etc. This card therefore advises you to make adjustments regarding the matter in question, to work things out with anyone involved. Try to arrive at equitable and mutually agreeable arrangements, taking the needs of others into consideration, hearing them out, and respecting differences—but stay mindful of what's negotiable and what's not. Be willing to make compromises and concessions in the interest of promoting harmony.

Because we all agree that the principles the Justice card represents are good things, it is difficult to determine how to emulate Justice reversed as a form of advice. However, there may be some situations, such as disputes between two wrong-headed or corrupted parties, where perhaps the best thing to do is to take after the Goddess Dike, who turned her back on the Iron Age race, disgusted with human crimes and hostilities, and fled to Olympus. There are certain cases where the law refuses to intervene in disputes because both parties are involved in illegal activities. For example, you can't sue someone for burning you in a drug deal, because both parties are said to have "dirty hands." If two parties are trying to draw you into a dispute, listen to both sides and consider whether this is a case of dirty hands, where the victimization is mutual. If so, this would be a situation from which to withdraw, like the aforementioned goddess.

Another form of withdrawal that is possibly advocated by the reversed card could apply to no-win situations: even though you may well be in the right, it may be preferable to back down in order to cut losses, save time and energy for more productive efforts, and/or to preserve peace and harmony.

There is an even more extreme condition to which Justice reversed may apply as an advice card; that is a situation where you feel you must lie, cheat, steal, or break other ethical or legal codes in the service of a higher cause. A historical example would be those people who conducted the Underground Railroad in defiance of the fugitive slave laws. I do not believe, however, that there are many situations in our modern lives where these kinds of actions would be justified. If you feel that you must compromise your integrity, be very, very, very sure that there aren't any alternatives you could take. Too often, people hurt their family and friends, and wound their own integrity, by rationalizing intricate excuses for doing shabby things— deceiving themselves and thinking that their actions are really necessary and in line with higher purposes.

XII
The Hanged Man

Rider-Waite Tarot

Legend Tarot

Celtic Dragon Tarot

XII: The Hanged Man

The Hanged Man card teaches us ways to put normal life in a state of suspension in order to gain peace and understanding. This card symbolically models different means to achieve this: by allowing oneself to be vulnerable, letting go of control, detaching from ego needs, practicing meditation and other techniques to step outside of ordinary consciousness, and by making voluntary sacrifices. Observe that the Hanged Man figure is usually portrayed with a tranquil expression, and is not very tightly bound to the pole from which he dangles.

When the Hanged Man comes up in a reading for advice, its meanings can be broadly applied: pause, refrain from action, detach yourself from the demands of the ego and the need to control what is happening, try to view your situation from different perspectives—and then, wait. If you are concerned about how to endure tough times and conditions, this card says, "Hang loose. Hang in there!" It implies that your problems are temporary. Be objective. Don't get personally involved or overwrought about the matter. It may be that things are in a transitional state, so it is not appropriate to do anything until something has crystallized, or at least until more information is gained. It may be that the thing you need most right now is a period of rest and reflection. Give yourself a chance to assess things, and allow some of the details of life to fall into order on their own.

If you are wondering whether to take action or make an important decision, generally, this card says "no," at least "not at this time." If the Hanged Man comes up when you are seeking advice pertaining to your projects, enterprises, and other general affairs, the Tarot advises putting them into a state of suspension. It is likely that the time is not good, or that there are other factors that need to be accounted for, things that need to materialize or mature before your work ought to go forward. Quite often, this pertains to actions or decisions that are in the hands of other people, so all you can do is wait.

However, if you have consulted the Tarot for help with creative problem solving, the Hanged Man may advise a need to look at your situation (or the matter in question) from new, even unusual perspectives. Sometimes it is necessary to put yourself in an unnatural position in order to jog the thinking process. This is also meaningful advice for those seeking insight and inspiration for art and other creative work.

Sacrifice is often associated with the symbolism of the Hanged Man, so if you've been considering the pros and cons of getting involved in an activity or relationship, the Tarot advises that you give generously and willingly of yourself, without expectation of reward. Don't expect a payoff, but view your efforts as an offering to the gods (or God). If you have consulted the Tarot about how to hang on to or recover a relationship or some other thing, it may be that you will just have to give it up and resign yourself to the loss. In this case, think of your sacrifice, your lost, loved object, as something that has been "made sacred" by having been given over to the gods.

The Hanged Man symbolism also implies trust and vulnerability, so in intimate relationships or human relationships generally, this card advises you to be less guarded and more willing to open up to others and let life happen to you.

There are times when we feel that nothing is really happening in our lives—at least nothing interesting or significant is happening in our outer lives—while we bide our time fulfilling some commitment or working slowly toward some far-off goal. However, when you draw the reversed Hanged Man card in an advice reading, the Tarot may be suggesting that if you alter your thinking, you won't have to feel that your life is on hold. Look for areas of life where you can find stimulation and enjoy growth, even if your outer circumstances are necessarily restrictive.

This card reversed in an advice reading may also call for you to limit some of the sacrifices you are making. Perhaps you have devoted yourself to something to the point of self-victimization, and now is the time to get back on your feet and stand up for your rights. Try to identify any areas of life where you have bought into victim consciousness, and try to turn these self-limiting beliefs around. For insight into the nature of your victimization, you can look to the house and sign positions of Neptune in your horoscope, if you have this information. These are areas where we can become so devoted to a cause that we allow it to overrun our personal boundaries.

Rider-Waite Tarot

XIII
Death

Sacred Circle Tarot

Golden Dawn Tarot

XIII: Death

Death is a complex card, for it depicts processes of destruction, dismemberment, and decay. In *Jung and the Tarot*, Sallie Nichols, an expert in Jungian symbolism, looks at the theme of dismemberment, noting that the severed heads, feet, and hands scattered in the field depicted in older versions of this card respectively denote the severance of old ideas, standpoints, and activities (p. 227). It's interesting, also, to reflect on the theme of decay, shown in versions where the skeleton is more cadaver-like, still having some flesh hanging to its bones. There is energy in decomposition, as the breaking down of matter produces heat, releases energy, and frees the elements to recombine and produce new life. In fact, this card hints at renewal and regrowth through the use of agricultural imagery depicting sprouts of life emerging from the field. The Waite version pictures Death crossing a river, signifying the need to move forward into the future, into a new state of being, a new way of life. Therefore, the Death card is about the process of change, not just about endings. The idea that change is necessary to prevent stagnation, and that Death opens a space for new growth, can have many implications in an advice reading. As always, do not be alarmed by the stark symbolism of this card, but consider your courses of action carefully in the context of potential interpretations and different circumstances.

For many of us, the most dreadful thing about death is not the prospect of pain and uncertainty, but the fact that it cuts us off from the people or things we love. Applied as a card of advice, the Death card suggests that you act the part of the Grim Reaper by ruthlessly eliminating something from your life, probably something related to the matter for which you seek advice. For questions regarding major life choices, this card advocates a complete change in lifestyle and personal status, and may indicate that some attachment is preventing you from moving into a newer, and possibly better, phase or way of life. If personal issues, attitudes, and addictions are throwing up roadblocks along your life path, harden your will and put yourself in "Terminator" mode, confronting these issues and working at dispatching them one by one. When I speak of acting out the Terminator, I refer to a visualization, a mental way of dealing with abstract issues; this is not meant to be a literal suggestion for dealing with human beings, and naturally, you should do nothing that would be hurtful to another person. However, for questions regarding relationships, this card suggests severing certain ties—presumably because the time has come to part ways. For example, there are rehabilitation programs that require their subjects to cut off contact with everyone with whom they associated in their old lives. These are extreme programs for extreme cases, but they illustrate the sense of finality associated with the Death card.

For questions pertaining to businesses, this card suggests consolidation: liquidate departments and projects that are not strong performers in order to get down to a leaner, more focused and efficient operation.

As a philosophical alternative interpretation related to the Death card's graphic image of the skeleton, the Tarot could advise that you detach from some of your peripheral selves in order to get down to a more essential Self. This is in accord with traditional interpretations that see this card as representing the death of the current identity. A person can have multiple selves that express multiple interests and relationships. Some of these selves are more like personas, which are social masks, while others are, on the continuum, quite deeply rooted and closer to what one may call a Core Self. Perhaps you have arrived at a point in life where there is a need for the figurative deaths of some peripheral selves, so that you can become more closely aligned with the Core Self—getting down to the bare bones, as it were. A hint at what this could mean is provided by Clarissa Pinkola Estes. In *Women Who Run with the Wolves*, she describes a legendary character called Bone Woman, who wanders the desert gathering up animal bones and then reanimating them. Estes sees the bones as representing "the indestructible aspect of the wild Self, the instinctual nature, the criatura dedicated to freedom and the unspoiled, that which will never accept the rigors and requirements of a dead or overly civilizing nature" (p. 35).

When you draw the Death card reversed, the Tarot may suggest that you deal with Death's issues on a more internal level, exploring its philosophical significance for you, and asking whether your way of life will lead, ultimately, to a meaningful death.

In acting out the Death card, along with the work of elimination is the work of mourning and letting go emotionally. The reversed card suggests that there is something in your life, such as a relationship or a certain phase of your existence, that is already effectively over and done with—except in your mind and hopes. Here, the Tarot advises that you give it up; acknowledge that it's over, mourn and grieve it for a while, and then move on into the next phase of existence.

XIV
Temperance

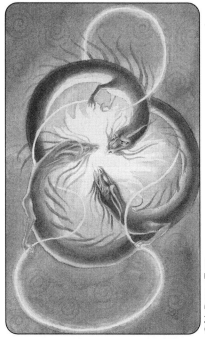

XIV: Temperance

The angel portrayed in the Temperance card is often seen as the individual's guardian angel, which some occult philosophies have identified as "the Higher Self." In this case, your personal mentor is your ideal you. Through the symbolism of Temperance, we can open a dialogue between ourselves and our spiritual templates. Through this interchange, we can discover what we need to bring into our lives to achieve health and wholeness. It is self-moderation that produces the self-esteem and genuine pleasure that derives from staying on our life paths and performing our dharmic duties with skill and competence.

Temperance has a lot to do with self-modulation in achieving the right blend of elements needed to enjoy physical, mental, and spiritual well-being. For each person, the "right" chemistry is different: it can take a lot of experimentation to find the ideal combination. Sometimes this involves integrating qualities, energies, activities, or things that are by nature opposite. Some of the opposing forces hinted at are: male and female, solar and lunar, active and passive, dark and light, conscious and unconscious, emotion and intellect, Apollonian and Dionysian, and heaven and earth. Take care not to equate these dualities. Although male and female, and good and bad are opposites, this does not mean that male equals good and female equals bad, or vice versa. The ingredients the angel mixes can be viewed as the various other influences that each person must bring into harmony, including the four elements (Fire, Earth, Air, and Water), the twelve signs of the zodiac, the functions of the conscious personality (feeling, thinking, sensing, and intuition), and so on. These elements are combined in new ways, resulting in new and creative ideas, insights, and products.

Temperance, like Strength and the Empress, is one of the Tarot cards that often relates to the needs of the body. These cards hearken to the old matriarchal values that teach that the body should not be despised, and that the details of physical existence are important. When body, mind, and soul are able to work efficiently and harmoniously together, the path of destiny becomes so much smoother. Temperance stresses moderation and self-management as a key to achieving this state.

When Temperance comes up in an advice reading, you must actively take control of your situation—quite likely by exercising more control over yourself. Self-discipline is part of the action called for. The self-management needed involves a process of experimentation that will require the expenditure of time and energy as you strive to find out what works for you. Here, any cards flanking the Temperance card will be significant: they show elements, qualities, or things you need to bring into your life routine (or reduce or phase out of your life, if reversed).

For general purposes, you can get some clues as to what constitutes your best mix by shuffling your Tarot deck and cutting it in any way you prefer; then, thumb through the deck until you find Temperance and the cards that go before and after it. Lay them out as a three-card spread with Temperance in the middle. If Temperance is reversed, set it upright; switch and reverse the flanking cards. Examine the meanings as well as graphic elements of the flanking cards for suggestions.

If Temperance appears when you are seeking advice for artistic inspiration or for overcoming creative blocks, it suggests bringing some new element into your project. Consider trying something with mixed media.

When Temperance appears in response to questions about job hunting, you may be advised to add a new skill to your repertoire. Take a chance on a creative resume that showcases a diversity of abilities, including things you may have overlooked as irrelevant to job requirements.

If you seek investment advice, Temperance recommends balanced funds that are diversified, mixing growth stocks with dividend-paying stocks or bonds.

If you seek advice on whether to pursue a relationship or what kind of mate you should look for, Temperance indicates a need for someone whose personality traits harmonize with, yet supplement, your own.

If health concerns are on your mind, Temperance advises you to take your health management into your own hands. Of course, you should also seek the advice of medical professionals, but this card tells you that your situation calls for very direct attention and awareness on your part. Therapies that involve the elemental powers of Water and Earth (as in mineral baths), attention to nutrition, taking in lots of fluids, etc., may be especially beneficial for you. There are some flower essences that aid the balance of elements that Temperance advises, including calla lily for the inner masculine and feminine, morning glory for achieving the optimum balance in lifestyle and daily routine, lotus for the synthesis of spiritual forces, and corn for the union of heaven and earth within.

In an ordinary Tarot reading, Temperance reversed may indicate self-undoing (due to an inability to integrate the elements of the psyche), but in a general advice reading, it tends to indicate that you are trying to micromanage everything. Here, it advises you to relax a bit, let go of control issues, allow situations to unfold naturally and take their own course, and delegate certain tasks to other people, where appropriate. In questions regarding health, Temperance reversed may indicate that you are too preoccupied with your health to be objective (perhaps to the point of hypochondria), so in this case you may be advised to worry less and find a health-care professional whose diagnosis and advice you are willing to trust.

Rider-Waite Tarot

XV
The
Devil

Golden Dawn Tarot

Celtic Dragon Tarot

XV: The Devil

In traditional Tarot interpretations, the Devil card is quite possibly the most negative card in the Tarot deck, representing bondage through addiction and other destructive or self-limiting behaviors. Interpreting this card for an advice reading, as suggesting actions to emulate, is rather problematic. However, I offer several alternative explanations, and you can consider whether one of them might apply to your situation.

Because the Tarot generally represents the Devil as a very nasty, frightening character, this card may come up when you are in a situation that requires you to be hard, even ruthless. Although most of life's problems are better handled through courtesy, communication, and negotiation, there are, unfortunately, some people, agencies, or forces who are impervious to reason and kindness, so being a nice guy will get you nowhere with them. This may especially be the case if you are dealing with swindlers, stalkers, or other members of the criminal element. In such cases, the Devil card may be telling you that tough measures are necessary for dealing with tough people or situations, and that you should do whatever is necessary to defend yourself and protect your interests. You may have to call on your own predatory instincts in order to thwart a predator. If the case is extreme and the danger imminent, self-defense may also include the use of baneful magic, or what the feminist witch Z. Budapest in *The Holy Book of Women's Mysteries* calls "the righteous hex." Budapest advises that hexes should be performed "only when you know, not just think, that someone has harmed you" (p. 75).

There are some things you have to do that are not evil or negative in and of themselves, or in their intent, but that will cause you to be perceived as a devil by other people. People tend to see as evil anything that imposes limitations on them, and the Golden Dawn system links the Devil card with the sign of Capricorn and its ruler, Saturn, the planet of limitation. In our society, many people have jobs or other roles that require them to enforce order and set limits, and in so doing, they earn the resentment of others. For example, no matter how much a teacher is concerned about students' self-esteem, there are times when he or she may have to flunk students who don't meet the standards. No matter how much a police officer may desire to use negotiation or other humane means to apprehend and calm a combative perpetrator, there are times when he or she may have to use extreme force. Thus, although we all may like to think of ourselves as good people and want other people to like us, the appearance of the Devil card may be telling us that now is not the time to be the nice guy. This may be especially true if we are normally hesitant to exert power over others, as a necessary part of our life roles.

A possible alternative interpretation for the Devil may apply to a common cliché: if you are in the situation of having to decide between two or more unattractive choices, this card may advise going with "the devil you know" as opposed to "the devil you don't know." In other words, choose in favor of whichever option you are the best informed about, or with whichever you have the most experience in handling.

Another possible application of the Devil card may relate to the two human, or semihuman, figures often portrayed standing before the Devil in a state of voluntary bondage. As a card of advice, this could suggest putting yourself in bondage to a cause or occupation—quite possibly something you hate—in order to achieve your purpose. This may not be much to your liking, but life sometimes presents us with situations in which we have to put very bitter limitations on ourselves that seem evil because of the hardships they impose.

Most versions of the Devil incorporate sexual and animal symbolism in their portrayal of the Devil and his minions, emphasizing this card's concern with animal drives. In an ordinary Tarot reading, this makes the statement that the indulgence of drives, which can be seen as servitude to one's body parts, is many peoples' most self-limiting factor. However, in an advice reading, the Devil may suggest a need to become reacquainted with your libido, which is an important source of energy and drive. This may especially be the case if you have approached the Tarot with concerns about low vitality or a loss of motivation. In the past, religious attitudes often forced people to suppress their sexuality, as well as other physical expressions; but in today's more liberal milieu, alienation from the body can still result from the unrelenting multitude of demands on the individual's time, and the nature of many peoples' work. These maladies are part of the modern condition, and if this is the case for you, the Tarot may be giving you permission to explore ways of refueling your drives and awakening your senses (providing you do not harm yourself or anyone else in the process).

If the Devil card comes up reversed in an advice reading, it may suggest the need to break addictions, limitations, and negative patterns—but perhaps through a policy of gradualism (e.g., the use of nicotine patches in trying to overcome smoking). There may also be a need to start loosening the bonds of a relationship, while still carrying out your responsibilities. This might apply to a work situation or familial relationship where you continue to fulfill certain duties, but have left the situation emotionally.

Reversed cards often urge you to look inward, and the reversed Devil card may suggest coming to terms with your shadow nature. The personal shadow consists of repressed materials, such as parts of yourself that have been disowned because their expression wasn't socially acceptable, or that would otherwise interfere with your ability to function on the terms of the work-a-day world. It is this talk of exploring the shadow nature that critics and other people who don't understand the deep spirituality movement find most alarming, so I must emphasize that this is not about unleashing "the axe murderer within," but rather, acknowledging to yourself that you do possess an array of dark urges, so that you stop projecting them onto other people, blaming the Other for all of the world's evil. Incidentally, there is also such a thing as "the positive shadow." Depending on our circumstances, some of us may have suppressed qualities such as courage, honesty, leadership, etc., and rediscovering these qualities is one of the heady experiences that comes with confronting the shadow.

Rider-Waite Tarot

THE TOWER.

XVI
The
Tower

16 THE TOWER

VORTIGERN'S FORTRESS

Legend Tarot

XVI   THE TOWER

Witches Tarot

XVI: The Tower

The desire to avert disaster is one of the main reasons that different systems of divination have developed. In the Tarot, the Tower card can represent the types of personal upsets and upheavals that most of us want to avoid. This is another card that looks bad in an ordinary Tarot reading, but has to be viewed differently in order to be interpreted as a course of action for an advice reading. Here, it tends to suggest acting on the symbolism in this card, which depicts a powerful force that changes a whole way of life.

With this card, there is always the recognition that as traumatic as changes may be, they bring about the necessary end to something that is unsatisfactory, whether in one's personal life, or in one's greater social environment. In Robert Graves' novel, *Watch the North Wind Rise,* he attributes necessary cataclysms to the dark aspect of the goddess, who proclaims, "When the water stinks, I break the dam. In love I break it." This philosophy may also be represented in the Tower, and leads us to recognize that when this card comes up, we are in the presence of the archetypal Goddess as Destroyer, who has been known as Kali, Tiamat, Sekhmet, and by many other names.

If the Tower card is about drastic, even catastrophic, changes, then the card read as advice to emulate suggests initiating such changes oneself. Quite often, things in life are in a state of not-rightness, and the situation deteriorates to where it can no longer be rectified through ordinary means. When this is the case, do some self-examination to determine where changes are necessary, and identify the obstacles to change. Changes usually need to be across the board. As a material construction that reaches toward heaven, the image of the Tower has both physical and spiritual implications; however, if you can make a fundamental change in attitude, it will be followed by significant changes in your physical world, and vice versa. When you are able to make these important changes, the Dark Goddess, or whatever you care to call this powerful force, won't have to make the changes for you.

Major and minor crises that start cropping up with alarming frequency are often warnings that something is out of whack in either your inner or outer life. The appearance of the Tower in an advice reading can be applied to Shekhinah Mountainwater's thoughts on such crises as "signals." She cautions, "A disaster signal is a warning that consciousness has been creating a certain combination of energies that are building up toward an explosion or cataclysm. The antidote is to change consciousness rapidly enough so as to alter the thoughtforms that are building toward danger." (For Mountainwater, who is a leader in the Women's Spirituality

Movement, the necessary changes are best achieved through goddess-consciousness, which can help mitigate social and ecological problems, and encourage more ethical ways to treat other people.) As part of the antidote to large-scale disasters, she suggests initiating "small-scale confrontations, such as admitting one's sexual preference, or pointing out oppressive situations firmly, but lovingly." Likening these confrontations to the minor temblors that can release stress along a fault line, thereby lessening the possibility of a major earthquake, she points out that although such confrontations "are risky and take courage to do (as they can create minor 'earthquakes'), they can, in the long run, prevent large-scale hostilities such as mass slaughter and war, or destruction on a more personal scale" (p. 205).

If you draw the Tower, you might consider whether you have been witnessing injustice, abuse, discrimination, or deception in your life or environment, and whether confrontation or some other form of truth-telling may be what is needed to help mitigate the problem. There may be a situation in your family, community, work life, etc. where you will need to act as a disruptive influence—perhaps as an iconoclast or whistle blower—even if such actions will affect your life or livelihood, or those of people around you.

Consider where drastic changes need to be made in your life. The Tower has a lot to do with the toppling of structures, so a restructuring, or even the total dismantling of certain systems may be in order. You must be flexible, imaginative, and prepared to let go of cherished beliefs and ways of doing things. If you are concerned about some project or enterprise, the appearance of this card indicates that it needs to be totally rethought or restructured. On the other hand, if you are in unsatisfactory relationships, especially if your partner or other important people in your life have problems with abuse, addiction, or infidelity, the Tower's advice is unequivocal: throw the bum out!

The Tower often refers to acts of God and other forces beyond our control, so if this card comes up in an advice reading undertaken because a crisis is already unfolding, it advises you to be flexible and go where the energy is taking you—presumably because your life has been in need of new directions.

When the Tower comes up reversed, the need for change is still indicated, but more restraint may be in order. Perhaps you could pursue a policy of gradualism and go about making changes in a discreet and nonconfrontational manner. The reversed card may also suggest finding a positive, but energetically expressive, way to vent your feelings or sublimate your energies.

XVII
The
Star

Rider-Waite Tarot

Witches Tarot

Golden Dawn Tarot

XVII: The Star

The Star represents a harmonious interrelationship between the things of the earth and the things of the spirit, depicting the energies that flow back and forth between the earthly and heavenly realms, promoting inspiration and growth. It tells us that we can access, and act as channels for, deep wellsprings of energy when we are able to model purity, simplicity, faith, and trust in spiritual guidance.

The Star is card number seventeen, which corresponds to the number eight because numerologically, seventeen yields one plus seven. In the Waite deck, which is the most widely used version of Tarot, the eighth card is Strength, but in older systems, card number eight is Justice. This makes an interesting connection between the Star and Justice, because Justice has been identified with the ancient Star Goddess Astrea, or Astroarche. In the Star card, this goddess presence provides a guiding ideal and promises help from deep spiritual forces. The image of the woman in the Star also has archetypal affinities with some Native American legends, as well as with the lore of Slavic, Teutonic, and many other peoples, wherein Star Maidens often mediate between the human tribe and heavenly beings, bringing gifts for human survival. The nudity of the Star Maiden portrayed in this card emphasizes her essential humanity, suggesting that we, too, can emulate her actions. One simple and basic way that we can do this is by extending blessings to others. The act of blessing involves the direction of life energy through good words (affirmations), good wishes (visualizations), and good deeds.

Let this knowledge inform your actions as you offer help, inspiration, and encouragement to other people. Extend blessings to all around you, and if there are some individuals who are giving you trouble—bless them as well. Do what you can to bless and help the natural world, too, just as the Star Maiden replenishes the gardenlike environment around her. Reflect on the concept that within everything is a spark of the divine, and seek to make connection with the soul-spirit in all people and things through the act of blessing. In blessing others, we are acting out the Star card, for as Elizabeth Roberts and Elias Amidon point out in their book *Earth Prayers*, "Through our blessings and invocations we acknowledge this network of forces that flows through the world, awakening the deeper levels of our consciousness to effect . . . patterns of change" (p. 170).

Wishing upon a star is also a tradition to which this card resonates, and the fulfillment of wishes is promised in the abundance represented by the countless stars of heaven and the lush environment and flowing waters pictured in this card. Applied as a card of advice, this suggests going after your dreams. As a form of imitative magic, a way to help wishes come true, find symbolic ways to act out your desires; find small ways in which you can start to lead the life you ultimately want to live. The Star's emphasis on trusting inner guidance would also advise you to trust luck by going after special opportunities that come up.

The Star can have special meanings for people in creative and inventive work. Fred Gettings comments in *The Book of Tarot* that the water jugs symbolize "the interchange of creative forces," while "the blue water suggests a malleable materiality which is the raw material of creative art." He goes on to discuss the star symbolism, pointing out that, "The graphic suggestion is that the stars and planets quicken inert matter, and that the resultant force, which is man, should in turn inject inert matter with life through making works of art" (p. 89). Thus, if you are already in some form of creative work, or are thinking about creative work, this card advises you to follow your dreams, to feel free to express yourself, and to make life and career choices in favor of options that will allow you maximum creative expression. If you are involved in some other line of work, this card would advise you to look for other ways to bring the creative and inventive elements into your life and work. Help generate the creative flow within yourself by associating with stimulating, creative people.

When the Star appears reversed, it suggests restraining some of the idealism the Star represents. You do not have to give up your spiritual strivings, but you may be in a situation that requires you to ground yourself and focus on more worldly concerns—at least for the time being. This also suggests relying more on personal resources than waiting for something magical to happen, based on the old saying that "the gods help them who help themselves." However, as you apply yourself to your business, have faith that things are destined to work out for you.

Rider-Waite Tarot

XVIII
The
Moon

Shapeshifter Tarot

Sacred Circle Tarot

XVIII: The Moon

The Moon is one of the most evocative cards in the Tarot, for its depiction of animals in an eerie moonscape can elicit some visceral reactions. The dog and wolf shown baying at the Moon represent our instinctual selves, although the dog represents the adaptations we have to make to get along in human society. In the foreground, a shellfish that emerges from a pool represents personal issues and expressions that have not yet developed, and that may relate to some very atavistic needs and aspects of the self. The water in which it swims is described by Eden Gray in *The Tarot Revealed* as "the great deep of mind stuff out of which emerges physical manifestation" (p. 95).

The Moon itself bathes the nightworld in its reflected glow while exercising creative and generative potentials over the creatures and landscape. Here, we are in the presence of the Moon Goddess Diana, described by one ancient writer as she who "presides over the whole of generation into natural existence, leads forth into light all natural reasons, and extends a prolific power from on high even to the subterranean realms" (Matthews, *Sophia, Goddess of Wisdom*, p. 61). Thus, we can see that the Moon card is about unconscious life and development. The older Tarot writers tended to see the Moon as a rather negative card because Westerners have often felt threatened when dealing with the realm of the unconscious. However, because of modern interests in exploring the riches of the unconscious, as well as in certain aspects of the Moon Goddess' personification of feminine wisdom, interpreters today view this card in a new light.

As a card of general advice, the Moon offers no clear-cut course of action, and indeed, indicates that this is not a good time to take decisive actions. The indications are that outer-world events are as yet unfolding, that there may be things going on behind the scenes that you don't know about, and that people and things are not what they seem, for appearances are distorted in the moonlight. Likewise, things are still in a state of development in your inner world. There is a push and pull on your moods and emotions, and choices are difficult because you are of a divided mind as long as deep issues are in contention with each other. You need to better understand your own motives for doing what you do, and determine whether you really want what you think you want. Because of the deep issues and underlying motives that are present, the appearance of the Moon card signals that this is a time for inner work. Set time aside for activities such as dreamwork, meditation, active imagination, psychoanalysis, and spiritual practice in order to sort out your motivations and desires. Associate with people who have done inner work themselves and can share insights.

One objective of doing inner work is regaining contact with your instinctual nature. Like the animals in this card, the animal within is especially helpful in two respects: finding nutrition and sensing danger. Because wild animals are generally able to discern which foods are suitable for them to eat and which not, this may serve as an analogy, encouraging you to gravitate toward activities, lifestyles, and people who will nourish your soul life by encouraging your inner expression. Utilize animal intelligence, too, by proceeding in an intuitive manner, trusting your instincts when it comes to making decisions, dealing with people, and so on.

When dealing with matters involving people, an understanding of the gentle, reflective nature of moonlight may be helpful in guiding your actions. Proceed quietly, discreetly, and cautiously, being sensitive and considerate of other peoples' feelings. This is a situation where emotional issues are very important, so to be persuasive, use the language of "feeling" people. If you are normally a "thinking" person, this will require a major effort on your part, and it may help to view the adoption of this new vocabulary and body language as an exercise in mental discipline. Also, this is not the time to dominate a situation; it may be better to lead by quiet example or work behind the scenes. Give credit to other people where appropriate, and cater to their egos if necessary.

Along with attention to intuitive messages, pay attention to the cyclic patterns of change in your life. The Moon may be advising you to arrange your personal affairs with respect to your natural cycles, and to consider how your life might better harmonize with the cycles of nature. This can apply especially to matters of physical and mental health, and suggests the use of natural therapies.

Because the Moon world in Tarot encompasses the world of nature, an alternative reading of the Moon as an advice card might suggest that you make decisions or choices that take you out into nature, or that at least allow you to live a life in closer attunement with nature.

The Moon is patron of romantics, eccentrics, and animals that don't come out during the day (often because they've been pushed into marginal habitats by humans), so the Moon also stands for the celebration of differentness, of otherness. Therefore, this card urges you to seek situations in which you can express your individuality and live your authentic self.

The Moon card's advice may also deal with the way we approach reality. In a moonlit landscape, you may feel like you are in another world, where fantasy and imagination spill over the boundaries of infinity. This means it may be necessary to do some reality testing. However, you can also use the Moon's ability to tinge the world with fantasy, in a positive way, by creating a unique learning environment for children, or by bringing more romance into a relationship, or by finding other ways to bring magic and mystery into your life. For people in creative work, this might be a good time to work with dream images.

The Moon card reversed may operate something like a dark moon or overcast night, where you have to proceed in the dark. This may indicate that your situation is one in which you must act without guidance; perhaps you will have to go forward with a plan or project without the desired information or preparation. It may indicate a need to keep a secret. You may have to deal with deceptions, distortions, and half-truths. If you feel the situation calls for it, you may need to conceal your actions or obscure certain truths from others, perhaps because the people you deal with would misconstrue your motives, or because the truth is too intense for them to handle.

Rider-Waite Tarot

XIX
The
Sun

Sacred Circle Tarot

Golden Dawn Tarot

XIX: The Sun

The Sun is a card of happiness, creativity, luck, growth, vitality, celebration, and affirmation. The Sun is also a teacher whose light is radiated outward and shared with others, whose energy and creativity nurtures and stimulates the growth of everyone who comes within his or her circle. An understanding of the Sun's influence on the world of nature helps inform our understanding of this archetype. An article in a 1948 issue of *National Geographic* that describes the sunlight as "the mother stuff of the universe" explains,

> The sun is the great mother. All life on earth might be considered as transient materialization of the exhaustless floods of radiance which she pours on the planet's surface. This enables green plants to synthesize sugars and starches from water in the soil and from carbon-dioxide gas in the atmosphere, thus making possible all other forms of life on earth by producing the essential foods. We eat sunshine in sugar, bread, and meat, burn sunshine of millions of years ago in coal and oil, wear sunshine in wool and cotton. Sunshine makes the winds and the rain, the summers and winters of years and of ages. Inextricably interwoven are the threads of Life and Light (Thomas R. Henry, pp. 343–44).

As a card of general advice, the Sun calls for enthusiasm, spontaneity, honesty, and genuineness in personal conduct. It favors all kinds of new adventures, activities, and enterprises, as well as creative work and self-expression. The Sun urges you to proceed confidently and openly as you act on your ideas and inspirations, and go after the things you want. It gives you permission to be exuberant, and tells you that you have a right to be yourself, to try something different, to draw outside the lines. Take the initiative and assume a leadership role. Don't be afraid to "toot your own horn," and let your light shine boldly. The Sun also indicates that you can enjoy success in any area that involves "firsts," whether for yourself or for society. If you have approached the Tarot with a direct question, the Sun is a card that says "yes."

When the Sun comes up in an advice reading, it urges you to turn on your inner light to permeate your being, and to radiate happiness outward. In this way, you can generate creative energy and promote the well-being of others, just as the sun promotes growth. Cultivate sunny thoughts as you hold in mind the words of Joseph Addison, who said, "Cheerfulness keeps up a kind of daylight in the mind, and fills it with a steady and perpetual serenity." If you have been suffering from depression and this is difficult for you, there are techniques for adjusting your attitude. One thing you can do is go through the motions, the actions, that a happy person would express. We often think that moods dictate behavior, but scientific experimentation has shown that it can also work the other way around: behavior can alter moods. Thus, when a person forces himself or herself to smile, the movement of the muscles involved in that smile actually trigger brain chemicals that produce a cheerful mood. Neuro-Linguistic Programming (NLP) provides its own techniques, teaching that when a person summons happy memories to mind, it actually boosts one's energy and competence. Other mental images can be made more positive by holding them in consciousness while casting them in a golden glow; negative thoughts may also be summoned, but then their images are consciously darkened and diminished. Of course, you can also boost your energy by reading comics and watching comedies. In keeping with the spirit of the Sun card, reach into dark corners and warm others with your radiance by hosting celebrations, visiting the sick and the depressed, helping the needy, and so on.

In many modern interpretations of the Sun, a joyous child is portrayed riding a horse; older versions feature two children dancing beneath the sun. The Sun card advises involvement with children and the things of childhood in response to questions about having children, working with children, and so on. Here, I would like to insert a piece of advice I read long ago, probably in a women's magazine. The author (whose name I didn't note) commented that she (or he) had noticed that the parents who turned out to be the luckiest in terms of having children who didn't rebel or get into other kinds of major conflicts, always beamed at their children. To beam is to smile in a very broad and open manner that signals unconditional love and acceptance. This is very much in keeping with the symbolism of the Sun.

Because the Sun card is identified with the joyous and playful energy of childhood, it can also pertain to the inner child—especially in the form of "the natural child" who is active, creative, inquisitive, spontaneous, and hopeful. Consequently, this card advises connecting with your inner child. Try to recall what you were like between seven and nine years of age, a time when your personality was crystallizing, but before you started conforming to the pressures of society. Reclaiming the natural child is a way of retrieving the "golden ball" that Robert Bly speaks about in *Iron John*. Describing how the action in fairy tales such as *Iron John* and *The Frog Prince* is initiated when the main character loses a golden ball, Bly says, "The golden ball reminds us of that unity of personality we had as children—a kind of radiance, or wholeness, before we split into male and female, rich and poor, bad and good. The ball is golden, as the sun is, and round. Like the sun, it gives off a radiant energy from the inside" (p. 7). In the process of growing up, you can lose that golden ball, and must seek it by pursuing the things—including the activities, people, places, ideals—that truly give you joy.

Another way of reclaiming the energy of childhood is rediscovering the creative potential of your Sun sign. In astrology, the Sun functions to encourage individuality and growth, to be creative and enable the individual to "shine" in areas for which he or she has a passion. Many of us learn about Sun signs when we're young, and it's exciting to know that this celestial power works through us and others who share our sign. After a while, however, we take the Sun sign for granted, and many of its expressive qualities become sublimated as we adapt to the needs of our social and work environments. There comes a time, though, often in middle age, when reclaiming Sun sign qualities can unlock sources of energy and happiness. If you have been in a situation that has prevented you from being yourself, your Sun sign can highlight the sort of activities that can enable you to break free.

Like the Moon, the Sun card has a lot to say about our relationship with nature, about being in a state of grace with nature and all its powers of growth, vitality, and fertility. If you have consulted the cards regarding your physical or mental health, the Sun's advice is obvious: you need to spend time outdoors, under the sun, getting some fresh air and exercise. Sunlight is an antidote to depression, and even more serious health problems can be somewhat mitigated by exposure to the sun, air, and nature.

The Sun can relate to the nature of the ego, so when this card comes up reversed in an advice reading, there may be an ego problem involved. Perhaps a case of ego inflation is causing you to take chances and overreach yourself. Your ego needs may be dominating other peoples' space to the point that you're causing them to wither. If you think that egotism may be the case with you, try to rein it in a bit; if you need to shine, do so with a softer light.

XX
Judgment

XX: Judgment

Judgment is a card about awakening to a Higher Consciousness, a state of awareness that allows us to recognize that we are truly spiritual beings within interpenetrating worlds of spirit. It is also about the states of grace and evolution for which humans may strive. Its illustration depicts people arising from the dead at the trumpet call of an angel. The angel is often identified with the individual's Higher Self, indicating the need for us as individuals to bring ourselves in line with higher purposes in order to achieve profound personal transformation.

Because radical spiritual transformation and expansion of consciousness is not something most of us can achieve overnight, interpreting Judgment as a card of advice for common situations requires a more modest and practical concept of transformation. One way that we can apply the advice of this card is by changing our attitudes and elevating our conduct so that we deal with matters as if we truly were highly enlightened beings. If we could put ourselves into the minds of people who are highly evolved, we wouldn't allow our moods or ego states to interfere with our responses, and we would make decisions based on the greater good, even if it went against personal interests. We would work for higher causes, and our interactions with other people would be guided by love, understanding, and compassion. We wouldn't worry about personal losses or setbacks because our minds would be set on the things of eternity, and we could see our role in the greater cosmic scheme of things. We can model ourselves after more enlightened beings by visualizing the lives and actions of historical or mythical figures who, though human, were able to act from these perspectives, which acknowledges our interconnectedness with the world of Spirit.

If you draw the Judgment card in an advice reading, it certainly calls for you to make some changes in your life. You can work toward spiritual self-betterment through meditation, prayer, devotions, and other practices that enable you to become more receptive to the voice of Spirit. Let all of your actions and decisions be informed by your recognition of the spiritual dimension of life. Since regeneration is a major theme of this card, you should also seek out the sorts of things that have a regenerative effect on you—especially spiritually inspirational things. This theme of regeneration may be especially meaningful for people in recovery programs, or who ought to be in recovery programs. General programs of self-improvement for mind and body can also help you to carry out this card's advice for transformation, for pulling yourself up to a higher level.

The sorts of changes recommended by this card may also involve rites of passage—phases of life often affirmed through social and religious rituals. These rituals involve a rebirth into a new identity and social role, and produce their own types of awakenings and transformations. Our society doesn't ceremonialize different stages and stations of life to the same extent as certain traditional societies do, but some passages that we do recognize and sometimes celebrate include marriage, programs of study, and military service. If you are thinking about committing to one of these life-changing institutions, this card would be in favor. Also, if there is a career or interest for which you feel "a calling," the Judgment card urges you to pursue it, even if it necessitates a change of direction or requires you to reject some material comforts.

In an advice reading, alternative applications of this card may relate to literal interpretations of the title word "judgment." It may mean that the situation requires you to make a judgment call, which is to say that it's up to you, and you alone, to make an important decision. Step outside of yourself, of your own emotions, prejudices, and conflicts, and ask yourself, "What is the most enlightened solution to this problem?" Then make the best decision you can with the information you have. Be confident and accept the consequences of your decision. Your call to action may include passing judgment on someone. Unless this card is surrounded by negative or unfavorable cards, it suggests promoting or rewarding him or her, taking into account this person's elevation, betterment, and individual needs.

When you draw the reversed Judgment card in a reading, many of the same meanings apply, but there is an indication that you need to look deeper inward, as well as backward, in order to prepare yourself for necessary changes. Look back over your life to assess where it has brought you, what you've been doing right, what you've been doing wrong, and what you need to do to raise the character and quality of your life to a higher level.

Related to the literal application of the term judgment, the reversed card may also suggest that you delay making a judgment, including judgments about other people, until all the facts are in, or until some looked-for transformation has been given more time to unfold.

XXI
The
World

Rider-Waite Tarot

Witches Tarot

Legend Tarot

XXI: The World

The World, which is the final Major Arcana card of the Tarot deck, stands for completion and portrays a dancing woman surrounded by the symbols of the worldly elements. It is interesting that after the profound spiritual transformations portrayed in the Judgment card, the Tarot takes the seeker's journey not into some etheric transcendental realm, but back to the world, to good old planet Earth. The message is that the self-realized person seeks right relationship with the things of the earth, within this planetary sphere, within this greater cosmos. This image evokes Walt Whitman's *Song of the Rolling Earth*, in which he avows, "I swear the earth shall surely be complete to him or her who shall be complete." It resonates to the Chinese concept that happiness and prosperity are attained when the individual internalizes the perfect balance of earth and heaven. We can view earth as the entire physical reality we have to work with, and heaven as the cosmic order. This ties in with Western Hermetic theories of the microcosm and macrocosm, the idea that the order of the universe can be seen as spheres within spheres that are mirrored, in fact embodied, within every individual. The World card makes the statement that with this knowledge, it is possible to achieve heaven on Earth.

As a card of general advice, consider the World's theme of completion: Ask yourself, "What do I need to be a complete human being, whole in mind, body, and spirit?" In a layout, the surrounding cards may suggest the other elements that need to be brought into your life. It's time to bring things full circle, so seek closure in your affairs, completing any projects, courses of study, or other matters in question, or perhaps even by completing a relationship with a wedding ring. Because the World calls for a celebratory mode of thinking and acting, affirm these accomplishments and the other good things in your life with a special ceremony or celebration.

Ideals of a personal world in a state of balance and completion also involve our ideas of life as it should be lived, so to help realize the promise of this card, visualize images of the beautiful life, active and exciting, aesthetic and gracious, whatever is the ideal for you, and act out your imagined life whenever possible. The ideal of the beautiful life is especially applicable to the creative life, which can achieve its own sense of self-containment, as illustrated in the words of Rilke, who said, "Take [your] destiny upon yourself and bear it, its burden and its greatness, without ever asking what recompense might come from outside. For the creator must be a world for himself and find everything in himself and in Nature with whom he has allied himself" (*Letters*, p. 19). These thoughts can help us integrate the symbolism of the World into artistic inspiration and creative living.

The symbolism of the World and its emphasis on quality of life can pertain to your personal environment, as well as to the larger environments we all share, in line with the metaphysical concept that putting things right in your own microcosm benefits the greater whole. The need to be in right relationship with the world around you calls for attention to your personal environment—not merely your living space, but your entire sphere of life, action, thought, and feeling. Louise Hay has a great affirmation of this in *You Can Heal Your Life*, "All is right in my world." Think about "right placement." Are you in the place you need to be, and doing whatever you can to create a harmonious personal environment and to promote a greater quality of life for yourself and those around you? Put your world in order so that it can be a regenerative space where you can build your personal power for effect on the larger world. Think about issues of inclusion and exclusion: what kind of people and things do you want in your world, and who and what do you not want? Work on expanding your spheres of influence and awareness.

Working on your personal environment, including your thought environment, has implications for larger spheres of life, including the well-being of the planet. In a metaphysical sense, when the individual is restored to wholeness, then Gaia Chthon, the imagination of the Earth, is also restored to wholeness. Therefore, the title and symbolism of the World card certainly pertains to global and environmental issues, so it advises thinking and acting with these things in mind. Be aware of what is going on in the world around you and try, whenever possible, to make it a better place. As a popular slogan goes, "Think globally, act locally." Take a biocentric approach, treating the community of plants, animals, and landforms as deserving equal consideration, with an equal right to exist. Consider also the human population by planning on a large scale, with thought to such things as the macroeconomic effect of your actions and their implication for future generations.

If you feel that a lot of things are wrong in your life and you draw the World card reversed, the implication is that the problem is with you, not with other people and outer circumstances. Therefore, the reversed card advises more attention to your inner environment. Alternatively, the reversed card may suggest that you limit your spheres of action, or that there may be a need to delay completion of something. Go back and take a second look at something you believe to have been completed.

Minor Arcana
Pentacles

Ace
of
Pentacles

Ace of Pentacles

Ace cards initiate issues related to the qualities and energies of their suit. For most people, the suit of Pentacles relates to material world concerns including money, prosperity, and security. When the Ace of Pentacles comes up in an advice reading, you are urged to examine the ways your beliefs and actions affect your ability to gain and maintain the resources you need to get beyond survival issues, free yourself from a number of worries, enjoy material and sensory pleasures, facilitate your aesthetic expression, and empower yourself to pursue your life's work.

To better understand the Ace of Pentacles, think about the qualities of gold, to which this card relates. Gold both attracts and radiates energy, as expressed in the saying, "Gold attracts gold." When used properly, when circulated, wealth has a self-generating quality, which we can relate to those old fairy tales about purses or tables that always replenish themselves. The distribution of wealth circulates energy that generates blessings. As in the parable of the talents, wealth must be spread around and put to work in order to realize its generative qualities.

As a card of advice, the Ace of Pentacles urges you to find productive uses for your money, goods, talents, time, energy, labor, and other resources, however great or small they may be. Whatever your concerns are, you should be prepared to put your money or other resources into them. If there is an idea or wish that you have been wanting to bring into reality, now is the time to start working toward it. If a business or investment opportunity has arisen, this card advises you to take advantage of it. Aces also deal with our work life, so this card suggests that you develop new skills and take on new jobs or material responsibilities.

Aces tend to give the go-ahead to whatever actions you are contemplating. If you see the Ace of Pentacles as advising the investment of a certain type of energy, then you can see that its appearance responds to questions beyond those dealing strictly with material concerns. For example, if you want to know whether or not to become involved in a relationship, this card says "yes," because any relationship (or any other type of commitment) requires you to draw on your time, energy, and resources.

The Ace of Pentacles advises you to focus on material issues. The having and using of wealth is liberating and empowering—consider how the word for wealth relates to *weal*, the old Anglo-Saxon word for well-being. If you are a spiritual or intellectual person who has been neglecting your material and financial well-being because you look down on material gain or feel that it isn't important, the Tarot is telling you that you have reached a phase where material expressions of empowerment are desirable. You may have to reevaluate your plans and actions so that attaining prosperity becomes a bigger priority. However, the prognosis here is favorable. As Louise Hay, author of the best seller *You Can Heal Your Life*, reminds us, "what we concentrate on increases" (p. 118), so the trend will be for accumulation, and abundance is assured.

To truly put wealth to work, one must be willing to take some risk, and cannot therefore be too attached to it. Indeed, one of the definitions of "capital" is money that is put at risk in the hope of reaping future rewards. In an advice reading, a reversed Ace of Pentacles may suggest that you spend more freely and loosen your grip on your holdings with this principle in mind. Naturally, we must use common sense in such situations so that we don't jeopardize our security; take care to know exactly what your assets and liabilities are, so you know how much you can afford to risk.

The reversed Ace of Pentacles may also indicate that you have been so focused on holding on to what you have that you have failed to recognize the needs of those around you, especially needs for material aid. In this case, you are advised to be generous with your time, labor, and substance in order to nurture your relationships.

Rider-Waite Tarot

Two
of
Pentacles

Sacred Circle Tarot

Celtic Dragon Tarot

Two of Pentacles

The Two of Pentacles concerns the need to balance responsibilities, as depicted in illustrations of this card showing a person trying to balance two disks. For many of us, this juggling act can involve time and energy put into career versus family. It can also represent seeking balance between our own needs and the needs of other people, public life and private life, inner- versus outer-world values, and so on. There are many other concerns we have to deal with, and people and situations that demand a piece of our time. This is the malady of the modern era, and it is addressed by Jon Kabat-Zinn, director of the Stress Reduction Clinic at the University of Massachusetts Medical Center, when he says in his book, *Wherever You Go, There You Are*, "A commitment to simplicity in the midst of the world is a delicate balancing act" (p. 70).

In advice readings, the Tarot cards are used to show actions we ought to take, so the Two of Pentacles suggests that you take on certain responsibilities in order to deal with a situation at hand. This card indicates that you are ready to make additional commitments, even if you have doubts. Stay calm and balanced. Two or more separate matters will make demands on your energy or attention. Try to give adequate attention to each, but deal with them one at a time, the best you can. Meet the multifarious challenges by drawing from all of the resources available to you (you'll discover some you didn't know you had). Since the Twos typically deal with the need to accommodate other people, prepare to do more for your loved ones, and others, too, even though this may result in some initial setbacks to your plans and goals. Wherever possible, try to simplify your lifestyle to better accommodate the duties you must undertake. Getting better organized can help you keep track of everything on your "to do" list and reduce your multitasking anxiety.

For many of us, the situation depicted in the Two of Pentacles represents our normal state of existence—always divided between one matter or another. In this case, the Two of Pentacles may make a statement about a philosophy of living. We tend to think that life is something that happens after we get all of our work and other obligations cleared out of the way. Unfortunately, that never happens. We have to see the act of balancing all our obligations and demands as part of the process of life, and learn to take a certain amount of pleasure in handling them competently and meeting these challenges one after another.

The Two of Pentacles answers affirmative to a number of questions, including those concerning the making of relationships, educational and career commitments, and so on, since these things naturally involve the assumption of many duties.

This card may also suggest a need to manage two separate lifestyles, identities, or occupations, as in the case of people who pursue two careers, or who maintain regular jobs while trying to start their own businesses.

When the Two of Pentacles comes up reversed in an advice reading, we might get a mental picture of the figure in the card being thrown off balance and dropping one of his disks. However, as advice to model, this may suggest that there is a need to shift attention from one or more of your responsibilities, at least for the time being, to give fuller attention to something else. Of course, this means that you may have to scramble to catch up on your other duties afterwards, but that is just something we all have to deal with now and then.

Three
of
Pentacles

Three of Pentacles

The Three of Pentacles denotes the personal expression achieved when creative energy is applied to the materials that Earth provides us. The results are joy in the creative process, pride in craftsmanship, and products of beauty and value.

When the Three of Pentacles comes up as your suggested course of action, consider the things to which you can apply your own creative energy. It doesn't matter whether you have unique skills or talents, nor do you need to have a gifted imagination. The emphasis here (at least for starting out) is on the process. Find an approach that enables you to express yourself. Give it your best, even if you find it challenging. This involves will: think about how to achieve an effect, get the materials you need, then invest the time and energy to carry it through. Take pride in your product because of the investment of energy, of self, that has gone into it.

Try to bring more of a creative and aesthetic element into your existing work, your daily work—whatever that may be. If your work does not seem to lend itself to an artistic touch, you can still strive to do it more perfectly, letting your skill and conscientiousness be your aesthetic. If your work goes unseen or unappreciated, think of your labor as an offering to the gods. Of course, the Three of Pentacles represents more than a work style—it can be a lifestyle, suggesting all of the ambient qualities of the creative life.

Since the Threes are cards of synthesis, you might consider bringing a variety of different elements into your creative work, or any other projects you undertake. For artists, this could involve mixed media; for others, it might suggest a mix of ideas and outside influences to stimulate new and productive thoughts or systems.

If you have approached the Tarot for advice on moving into a more rewarding and meaningful job, this is a good card to emulate. As a form of imitative magic, pursue a hobby or do some volunteer work that is of the same nature as the type of work you would like to get. Traditionally, this card predicts creative success, and is an affirmation of the principle that when people really put love and care into their work, there will be a demand for their services. Therefore, this card's advice applies to questions about seeking abundance, fulfillment, acclaim, and right livelihood, and embodies the principle named in the title of Marsha Sinetar's book, *Do What You Love, The Money Will Follow*.

The Three of Pentacles recommends things you can do with your hands, particularly if they give you the joy of forming something out of raw materials. When we're working creatively, there's a state of flow, a state of grace. There is magic in the media, especially when you're working with natural materials. Note how becoming involved in an art or craft, or doing any kind of work with the focus and reverence of a true craftsperson, creates the feeling of inner focus and spiritual well-being that gives us a sense of connection with the Higher Powers.

To apply the Three of Pentacles, work on your attitude so that you see yourself as being fully and permanently in the employment of the Higher Powers (or God, Goddess, Deity, the Living Universe—whichever term you prefer to use). Take the attitude that the Higher Powers will always support you, while putting you into better and better positions. Affirm, also, that there will always be someone out there who needs your own unique combination of character, skills, and experience.

In an advice reading, the reversed Three of Pentacles may suggest a need to loosen your standards somewhat. Because we acknowledge the importance of diligence and good craftsmanship, this is hard to accept, but there are some situations that may warrant it. Perhaps you are investing too much creative energy, indeed too much of yourself, in some matter or enterprise that is yielding diminishing returns or depleting your resources. The popular term "good enough for jazz" may reflect the attitude you need to take here.

Rider-Waite Tarot

four
of
Pentacles

Witches Tarot

Celtic Dragon Tarot

four of Pentacles

When the Four of Pentacles comes up in an advice reading, you are encouraged to focus on material issues and material things. The symbolism here is quite solid, as both Pentacles and Fours represent the qualities of earth, matter, and materiality.

Among spiritually oriented people, there is a certain prejudice against the accumulation of money and material wealth, and that is even reflected in the graphic depiction of many versions of this card. Often, the figure in the Four of Pentacles card is shown as a rather mean and miserly looking sort of person, and interpreters respond to this card rather negatively. Despite the fact that we may look down on the miserly figure, material security is certainly an important factor in self-empowerment. Money can give a person a greater amount of personal freedom—especially freedom from a number of worries—and people who disdain material concerns can run into problems because they fail to build a financial safety net. However, the acquisition of goods does become a problem if a person is obsessive about it, trampling on others, ruining his or her health, and obstructing the growth and health of relationships. If materialism and materiality are issues for you, consider whether you view material accumulation as a means or an end to your goals.

Using the Four of Pentacles as a card of advice, we might follow the example of the individual pictured in the card, despite what different Tarot artists and interpreters might think about him as he defensively clasps his pentacles, coins, or disks. This card advises you to cultivate your own resources, hang on to what you have, and provide for your old age and future security. This is the case especially if you have consulted the Tarot about whether or not to loan money or give something away. If you have been beset with demands from friends or relatives for your time, money, or substance, this card is urging you to be a little more selfish; this is a time when it's important to look first to your own security. Take good care of your material possessions, making sure that they are protected and maintained in good working order so that they will last as long as possible.

The symbolism of the Four of Pentacles also relates to enclosed spaces, so this card advises you to spend more time at home. Claim a room of your own, or some other personal space. Put more energy into your home, and do what you can to make it more secure. Related to the stolid earth symbolism in the Four of Pentacles, this card also recommends grounding activities as an antidote to nervousness, depression, spaciness, loss of personal focus, or other types of mental and physical problems. Do relaxing, rhythmical things (such as crafts or certain types of home maintenance activities) that allow you to work with your hands and with the things of the earth.

Reversed cards represent a loosening of a card's qualities. As an advice card, the Four of Pentacles reversed suggests that you unload things that are weighing you down. Perhaps it has gotten to the point where caring for your property is draining your time and energy, or preventing you from getting out for more active and creative pursuits. In business and finance, this reversed card may recommend consolidation: dispose of interests and investments that are less fruitful, and concentrate on the proven winners in order to make life simpler. In personal relationships, this card may recommend being freer with your time and energy. Perhaps you have been withholding something from those close to you who genuinely need and deserve your generosity. The reversed Four of Pentacles also pertains to a values shift, challenging you to redefine your values. Decide what kind of material things you want in your life, and how much value you want to place on them.

five
of
Pentacles

Rider-Waite Tarot

Celtic Dragon Tarot

PENTACLES **5** PENTACLES

Material Trouble

Golden Dawn Tarot

five of Pentacles

Having the Five of Pentacles come up as a suggested course of action in an advice reading is apt to be perplexing. The things this card represents are not normally welcome, especially in view of the dangers of "poverty thinking." However, the Five of Pentacles can offer some tough wisdom, advising you to let go of your attachments and to live more simply. This does not mean that you should subject yourself to the most extreme conditions pictured in this card, but it may be a good idea to impose some austerity measures—especially if you have not been doing the best job of saving and economizing.

Even if you have not been profligate in your habits, and your general situation is fairly secure, the Five of Pentacles may advise that you temporarily act and think as if hardship were threatening. The trick here is to see it as a game: hold to the idea that you really are a person of resources, but are temporarily subjecting yourself to these measures as a form of test or discipline. Make this an opportunity to find pleasure in simpler things. See if you can save more money each week than you did the week before. Make a project out of budgeting by researching the things people did to get by during the Depression. For example, if entertainment is a major expense for you, find out what families did for fun in the Depression, or in other simpler eras. You could read books on subjects like homesteading to find out how people who live close to the land find ways to make do.

Because economic reforms often take time to implement, the Tarot is probably suggesting that you live austerely for a fairly substantial length of time. You'll have to use your intuition to determine how much, and for how long, you should economize, and check back with the Tarot from time to time for further advice. When you feel you have done enough to satisfy the requirements of this card, reprogram yourself with a cleansing ritual—perhaps a luxurious bath—then listen to tapes or read a book on "prosperity thinking."

In an ordinary Tarot reading, the appearance of the Five of Pentacles indicates that it's a bad time to make changes, start risky enterprises, or make investments. However, advice cards are read somewhat differently, with the scene depicted as suggesting a certain course of action. Therefore, this card may advise that you find some new applications for your energies and resources, even if it involves risk-taking or lifestyle changes. It could also suggest putting your money at risk in speculation or other types of investments.

On the other hand, there are situations in which this card may be advising you to "cry poor." Perhaps you need to resist your child's request for a sixty-dollar video game, or turn down a relative who is asking you to post bail. Where relationships are concerned, this is a card that advocates a policy of tough love.

If you seek guidance on spiritual self-betterment, the Five of Pentacles suggests submitting yourself to a period of simplicity, renunciation, and abstinence. It may be that you have to put up with some physical discomfort in order to gain more personal spiritual rewards.

This card may also suggest that you be mindful of the problems of others and deal with the poor and oppressed on an empathic level. Perhaps your spiritual growth will be aided by engaging in some kind of volunteer work where you can help the afflicted in a very direct and personal manner.

When the Five of Pentacles comes up reversed in a reading for advice, there is an indication that survival issues may dominate your thoughts to the extent that they are blown out of proportion. A more realistic assessment of your situation is needed. If you frankly consider your worst-case scenarios, you'll find that your problems would still be manageable.

The reversed card also points to a need to take on burdens while being careful to avoid poverty thinking. Be aware that poverty can be seductive! Some people limit their own aspirations as a way to escape personal responsibility. To cite a common example: a person finding himself or herself laden with debts or burdens pleads hardship to get out of them—and then permanently incorporates neediness into his or her lifestyle rather than saying, "Okay, this is my responsibility, so I'll economize, work harder, and do whatever else is necessary to manage the situation." If this applies to you, you must make a turnabout and assume your obligations and honorable debts.

Rider-Waite Tarot

Six of Pentacles

Witches Tarot

Legend Tarot

Six of Pentacles

The Six of Pentacles denotes a measure of peace and prosperity that is attained through work and thrift; this results in a shift of focus to the quality of daily life. People who reach this stage may find that they can finally put some of their worries about security behind them and begin to enjoy life. At such a time, many feel the desire to share some of what they have, to use their resources to benefit others, so this card often portrays a rich man handing out coins.

When the Six of Pentacles comes up in an advice reading, the Tarot may be calling for your generosity and openness, emulating the popular illustrations of this card. If someone has asked for your help, this card says, "Yes, you should give of your time, energy, and substance." If you have not actually been approached with a request for help, look around to see if someone near you has a pressing need that you are in a position to help alleviate. If you do decide to help people, it is important to be sufficiently attuned to their needs to give them the things they can genuinely make use of. Too often, we're likely to offer the sort of things or services that we value ourselves. Although it is laudable to have a generous spirit, our help may not be of the sort that is most needed. Of course, generous impulses must be guided by common sense with respect to what you can afford to give. In most graphic depictions of the Six of Pentacles, the man who is handing out charity holds a pair of scales. This serves to remind us that how much we can give to others must be balanced against our personal needs and resources, and must be meted in a way that does not create dependency.

The generosity associated with the Six of Pentacles can have broader applications too, depicting our duties toward our fellow humans, collectively. When we reach a certain level of maturity, success, and social awareness, we recognize that the act of giving something back to society is something a responsible person does. We also come to realize the need to give something back to Mother Earth. The Six of Pentacles is associated with the Earth element. Giving back pertains not just to monetary donations, but to giving of our time as well, which is truly one of our most precious commodities. This service ethic is promoted by Hilary Rodham Clinton in *It Takes A Village,* where she emphasizes that "compassion and empathy are more likely to take root if they are grounded in daily life," and that we can condition ourselves to view service as "not only an obligation but a privilege" (p. 194). The habit of giving back is also personally empowering. This sense of duty is not limited to people of higher income: many low-income people are proportionately more generous than those better off, and instill a sense of empathy in their children.

Because Six cards represent periods of relative ease and have aesthetic associations, the Six of Pentacles also hints that now is a good time to put your material resources to creative uses. This card promises success for artistic efforts, as well as certain types of businesses and investments. You can carry this energy further by finding ways to bring things of beauty into your daily life and setting time aside for earthly pleasures.

Sixes also represent cycles and circulation, so this card can pertain to situations where you are advised to get out and around, to spread your influence. If you think the time has come to look for a better job, circulate your resume.

If you draw the Six of Pentacles reversed, the Tarot may be suggesting that you help others, but within certain limits. It may be necessary to give sparingly, or to control or put conditions on what you give. For example, if your children are asking for money or other privileges, you might set up a system of points where they can earn certain amounts in exchange for doing chores or homework.

Seven
of
Pentacles

Seven of Pentacles

When the visionary number Seven is grounded in the practical suit of Pentacles, the result is a desire to bring our dreams and aspirations into material reality. In order to take the steps necessary to materialize these goals, we must be fully committed to carrying things through, be prepared to invest time, energy, and even money, and be willing and able to work for delayed rewards. We must also have the imagination to visualize what is possible (and desirable), the type of growth involved, and the foresight to think ahead to what to do next and what will be needed beyond that. This card is a teacher who embodies the wisdom of the person who works close to the earth, does things in a timely manner, and cultivates patience with the understanding of how things must grow with the progression of the seasons.

When the Seven of Pentacles comes up in an advice reading, you are urged to invest your time, energy, and resources in plans and projects that offer future prospects of material rewards. Along with this, you must form a practical plan for taking things on a step-by-step basis. If you've been thinking about starting a business, making an investment, going back to school, getting special training, or starting any other project to which you are prepared to devote yourself patiently, this card encourages you to commit yourself to it. Generally, all actions must be taken with the future in mind. Be prepared to deal with some risk (with the Sevens there's always an element of chance), as well as a period of waiting and uncertainty. Believe in yourself, and have faith that your efforts will come to fruition. Be sure to maintain a positive attitude. You can't feel that your life is on hold while you're waiting for something to happen, so plan some diversions and maintain an optimistic outlook to help you bide time. Continue to visualize the fruition of your goals, and sustain your vision by reading inspirational literature and seeking encouragement from people who believe in you.

Some Tarot interpreters believe that the Seven of Pentacles has astrological affinities with the planet Saturn in Taurus. This means that this card would favor enterprises that involve working with the earth, such as agriculture or mining, and also things that deal with material structures, such as construction. This card also favors futuristic ideas that integrate traditional values.

If you have approached the Tarot because you are concerned about the outcome of some action or endeavor that you have already taken, this card assures you that if you've done the proper preliminary work (i.e., sown the seeds, laid the foundations, set the machinery in motion), you may now relax and stand back, though you should continue to keep an eye on the growth of the matter in question.

For parents concerned about the development of children, the Seven of Pentacles advises you not to worry, but to allow them to mature at their own pace. However, this card is in favor of good nutrition and other programs to encourage the healthy growth of children. It also advises allowing relationships, investments, and other matters to grow at their own rate.

When you draw the Seven of Pentacles reversed, this card may warn you to anticipate complications. You will need to deal with them expeditiously, so be watchful. The aforementioned Saturnian association calls for a certain tough-mindedness in dealing with potential problems or weak performers: nip problems in the bud, and don't allow anything to go to seed. The reversed appearance of this card may also be suggesting that there is a need to be more flexible, less fixed on the outcome of your plans. The Seven of Pentacles' emphasis on patience and planning advises you to allow for some losses.

I once read an old Indian saying that referred to the planting of seed; it went something like, "One for the squirrel, one for the crow, one for the worm, and one for me," acknowledging that we have to accept some loss as part of the way of nature. This is the attitude you may have to take. Be assured that if you plant enough seeds, some will eventually bear fruit. Don't put all of your hopes into one thing, and be willing to change your plans if things start to look like they are not going to work out. Make contingency plans that include alternative courses of action. If the reversed Seven of Pentacles is followed by cards of action, it may suggest that you act quickly to prevent losses; if by cards of retreat, think about cutting your losses.

Rider-Waite Tarot

Eight
of
Pentacles

Shapeshifter Tarot

Legend Tarot

Eight of Pentacles

The Eight of Pentacles is a card about applying yourself, especially by getting your stuff together related to the Pentacles concern with personal resources and material accumulation, and the number Eight's symbolism of stability and balanced organization. As a card of general advice, the Eight of Pentacles tells you to work on the organizational details of any matter in question. It calls for skill-building and pride in craftsmanship and ownership as you organize, care for, and maintain your materials and resources. It provides logical follow-up for the Seven of Pentacles because there can be a great degree of uncertainty in waiting for long-range plans to materialize. By organizing your things and concentrating on craftsmanship, you can shift focus to the present. The Eight of Pentacles also exemplifies a mode of thinking and acting that can help daily life run more smoothly, whether at home, in the workplace, or in other areas of life. When we are able to organize and properly maintain our work materials and our personal possessions, we create an ordered space in which it is possible to enjoy greater productivity and personal performance. This frees energy and adds to our quality of life.

This card applies especially to vocational issues. The illustration for the Eight of Pentacles, which shows a young apprentice working on his craft, has meaning for people with questions pertaining to education, career planning, job hunting, and creative work. It suggests a need for more skills and advises entering a course of training that involves discipline, values of craftsmanship, and mastery learning. Base a practicable program for further self-development and purposeful labor on a realistic self-assessment, using the knowledge that has come from your life's experiences. Organize your material resources to support your goals. For job hunters, be sure to mention in your resumes, applications, and cover letters any special training you have undergone, and emphasize that you have a craftsman-like attitude toward the work you undertake. The Eight of Pentacles' attention to quality and immersion in process also enhances self-esteem because much of our personal identities are tied up with our work and our possessions (especially our own handiwork). In *Grasping Things*, Simon Bronner quotes Emerson's observation that "a man coins himself into his labor; turns his day, his strength, his thoughts, his affection into some product which remains a visible sign of his power" (p. 115).

For business owners, the Eight of Pentacles may advise the purchase of equipment and organizational supplies for the office, or the implementation of training systems to promote greater efficiency.

For parents, it suggests a need to supply children with a quiet study area and a demonstration of the values of concentration by turning off the TV and studying alongside the kids. It may also suggest deferring more abstract studies in favor of vocational programs or other types of activities that involve working with the hands, which have a focusing effect on young people.

For those who seek creative inspiration, the Eight of Pentacles suggests that your problem is less with inspiration than application. Remember Thomas Edison's words to the effect that invention is one percent inspiration and ninety-nine percent perspiration. If you can't think of anything brilliant to do, just go through the motions to get yourself busy, and try to work your way through your creative block. (I find that when I experience writer's block, the act of organizing my notes and files magically helps to get the creativity flowing again.)

In questions pertaining to relationships, the Eight of Pentacles may suggest a need to work at preserving and enhancing your relationships with loved ones and others.

This is also a card about having something to do. In Air Force survival training, there is a saying that goes, "When you don't know what to do, do something." By doing something, anything, rather than panicking or dithering, you become calm and focused, and accomplish something besides. This wisdom doesn't apply only to survival situations, it can help us deal with many of life's circumstances. If you have approached the Tarot with questions about how to bide time, get through a fallow period, cope with stress, ease loneliness, or deal with difficult, unpleasant, or chaotic situations, the Eight of Pentacles suggests that you simply look around for something to do. Organizing your possessions or immersing yourself in other maintenance activities can be just the thing to divert your attention from problems. If you are in a panic because you have lost or misplaced something, you're often likely to come across it while cleaning out other things.

In an advice reading, the Eight of Pentacles reversed would suggest investing less energy in a certain plan, program, or course of study, or in the maintenance of property or collection of objects. Perhaps your efforts are yielding diminishing returns, or the probable payoff just isn't worth it. The Eight of Pentacles may also suggest that you invest less of yourself in your work life and identity. Perhaps your employer doesn't appreciate the extra work you do, or you are in a situation where working harder is no insurance against layoff. The reversed card may also hint that you are wasting too much time on preparation and other details for a project or venture, suggesting that you have attained the necessary competency and now is the time to become more actively involved, whether or not you feel you are sufficiently prepared.

Nine
of
Pentacles

Nine of Pentacles

The Nine of Pentacles is about using your resources to create a beautiful lifestyle and expressing your values through your way of living. This card is auspicious in that it indicates you have reached, or are about to reach, a financial and emotional state where you can live life on your own terms—and that the universe will support you in your endeavors. This may indicate that you will be able to live a very gracious lifestyle, but it may just as well betoken a way of life that is remote, creative, eccentric, free-spirited, or offbeat, if any of these alternative lifestyles represents the ideal for you. If you are trying to make a decision about what to do with the rest of your life, especially if you are facing retirement, an empty nest, or the possibility of pursuing a second career, this card urges you to do something you enjoy, and to do it without guilt. Don't concern yourself with whatever society or the people around you think you ought to do with your time.

Perhaps you have worked so long to raise a family or to meet the other contingencies of living, working, and getting along in the world, that you have forgotten just what it is that you would really like to do. In this case, it may be necessary to do some deep thinking: try to remember what ideas energized you in the past, and to visualize what sort of life would be most meaningful and pleasurable for you. This card especially suggests that the activities or choices that will give you the most fulfillment are the ones that allow you more solitude and an opportunity to live more of the inner life. If you are thinking about working at home or becoming a homemaker, this card would be in favor of it. The Nine of Pentacles is especially likely to come up as an advice card when you have been succumbing to the pressures of a society that views introversion as an abnormality, or the resentment of family members who may be threatened by your literal or figurative desire to have "a room of one's own." While admonitions to get out and be more active in the world may be good advice for other people in other circumstances, it may be that, at least for the time being, the path you need to follow is an inward one—especially if you are trying to achieve self-regeneration or to lead the creative life.

Along with its emphasis on the right to claim your own space, this card also urges you to use your time and substance as you see fit, without guilt about enjoying the fruits of your labors, surrounding yourself with beauty, or indulging in such luxuries as you can reasonably afford.

There is an alternative meaning for the Nine of Pentacles: although this card generally represents abundance and the creative enjoyment of material resources, its popular graphic depiction of a solitary woman and its association with self-sufficiency have led some Tarot readers to interpret it as indicating a comfortable but solitary existence, as, for example, widowhood or spinsterhood. In an advice reading, there are some special circumstances to which this particular interpretation may be applied: if you have been experiencing anxiety about being single, perhaps worried about growing old alone, this card may suggest that you reconsider the single life and look for the positive things your independence allows. This does not mean that you have to abandon the hope of achieving a lasting relationship and being surrounded by loved ones, but it does indicate a need to attain self-sufficiency and come to terms with the possibility of being alone. The Tarot may foresee that at some point you will be glad you're capable of self-reliance. It might be helpful to bear in mind that members of the opposite sex are more attracted to people who are independent and have cultivated talents and outside interests, and they are turned off by people who are too dependent. Also, consider ways that it may be possible for you to live independently and yet maintain passionate and fulfilling relationships.

When this card comes up reversed, it suggests that while solitude and self-sufficiency are important to your self-expression and quality of life, there is a need, at least for the time, to venture out more, become involved in some outside activities, and allow yourself to interact with and rely on other people. It may be that more outside contact and input is what you need to boost your creative productivity. If you are by nature an introvert (perhaps even somewhat agoraphobic), extroverted activities will enable you to activate one of your "inferior" functions, which is an effective way to access unconscious wisdom and experience serendipitous events. Seeking outside experiences need not be intimidating. You can try to do things on your own terms by selectively engaging in activities that are pleasantly stimulating, but not overly stressful for you, such as traveling to acquire beautiful things to bring back to your home. The reversed card may also suggest sharing your quality of life, perhaps through patronage or other means of encouraging loved ones or other worthy people to craft creative lives, too.

Rider–Waite Tarot

Ten
of
Pentacles

Witches Tarot

Legend Tarot

Ten of Pentacles

The Ten of Pentacles is a card about the use and accumulation of family resources and the responsibilities that go with them. The resources in question can be material and financial, as the Ten of Pentacles generally refers to a family's collective wealth and security, and the material aspects of the family support system. However, this card may also refer to the human resources we have access to as members of extended families that can offer moral and emotional support as well as a pool of knowledge, skills, talents, and experiences. Family capital may also refer to heritage resources, such as the sense of inclusion, solidarity, and identity that emanate from shared experiences and traditions.

Generally, as an advice card, the Ten of Pentacles suggests that you focus on building family stability, security, and well-being—especially with regard to financial and material conditions. This may suggest a need to be generous to family members—including those in your extended family. However, other things that strengthen the family's infrastructure, such as the establishment of certain traditions, will also contribute to the idealized situation this card portrays. You should involve all generations of your family and reach out to include your more distant relations, too. This card also urges you to make decisions and choices that promote the well-being of your family or group, placing collective needs ahead of personal desires if necessary. Don't do anything that would compromise your family's reputation, but work to improve its standing in the community. If there is a problem with the division of family property or inheritance, the Ten of Pentacles advises you to think in terms of the greater good, dividing things fairly with the understanding that the prosperity of the extended family promotes a stronger network that benefits everyone.

If you need help with a matter in question, whether emotional, financial, or otherwise, this card advises looking to your family and extended family network for help. It implies that your family has the resources you need. Think about how you can later add something to your family's resources by way of repayment. If you are looking for a job, or trying to decide on a job, there is a possibility that your best opportunity may come through creating or joining a family firm—or at least by broadcasting your need, by word of mouth, through your family network.

With the material abundance shown in this card, there is also an implied abundance of responsibility because caretaking is a major concern of the Pentacles suit. For most of us, these major material responsibilities are apt to be related to our family obligations. Thus, the Ten of Pentacles may show the benefits coming from your extended family support system, but it also indicates that you must have an active role in maintaining that network of relationships and care. Therefore, the Ten of Pentacles suggests that you practice kin-keeping techniques, which can involve writing and phoning extended and distant family members in order to keep the lines of communication open and prevent people from drifting away; anticipating and helping out with other members' material needs; acknowledging members' issues, ideas, and concerns; showing up to show polite support of others' milestone celebrations such as anniversaries, home movies, recitals, etc., even if they aren't of absorbing interest to you; and making special efforts to give encouragement to the young. If you have been asked to take on a responsibility or obligation pertaining to the maintenance of family relations or family property, this card urges you to accept it. The Ten of Pentacles is also in favor of taking on the care of your elderly parents or assuming custody or guardianship of children.

In keeping with the Tens' concern with new generations, this card may also suggest mentoring young people around you by sharing your resources, values, and experience. Think about other ways you can leave a legacy for the future. Make sure you have a will, a living trust, or other provisions for passing on your property.

The reversed Ten of Pentacles may suggest finding ways to honor your family ties while moving in new directions, founding new traditions, moving into new social and occupational categories, and defining new values. A reversed reading may also suggest that while you should make the well-being of family a priority, it may be advisable to withhold your generosity, or at least put heavy conditions on it, if people with a poor record of responsibility are seeking your help. It may also suggest a need to avoid, or even exclude, troublemakers who threaten the family's stability.

Page
of
Pentacles

Rider–Waite Tarot

Celtic Dragon Tarot

Witches Tarot

Page of Pentacles

When you draw the Page of Pentacles in an advice reading, you are urged to explore material world qualities and values through learning situations that incorporate new responsibilities. Sometimes this may mean going back to school or finding a new line of work. Learning by doing usually involves trial and error, so don't be afraid to make mistakes—it's all part of the process. The Tarot may also advise finding a dedicated, practical-minded friend with whom to share your learning experiences.

The Page of Pentacles needs to gain skills, experience, and responsibilities by working, so this card advises you to put yourself in a position where you can work and learn at the same time. Of course, one of the great Catch-22s of the would-be worker is that no one is willing to hire someone without experience, and it is hard to get the right kind of experience without having had the opportunity to work. One of the best solutions to this problem is to first do volunteer work related to your area of interest. Volunteer organizations can't afford to be picky about accepting untried people, and they often provide mentors who are willing to spend time with you and are able to show you the ropes. Volunteer service also looks good on resumes because it denotes a person with a deep level of commitment to the community.

Generally, the Page of Pentacles advises against taking action or getting involved in an activity until you can give the matter more study or come up with a better plan, especially if you have approached the Tarot with a question about investments or management concerns. However, this card is very much in favor of apprenticeship-type programs and other learning situations. Pentacles often deal with money and business matters, so the Page card may here advise learning more about your finances and household affairs.

The Pentacles suit is connected to Earth, so the appearance of this card may also advise you to reeducate your senses. Achieve greater familiarity with your surroundings. Explore nature with childlike openness and inquisitiveness, and think about the ways nature relates to the four ancient elements of Fire, Earth, Water, and Air. Experiment with new things that give you physical or aesthetic pleasure. If you have been too focused on spiritual or intellectual pursuits, you may discover that refocusing on things you can see and touch can be quite rejuvenating.

An important Page of Pentacles task is to devise work routines that will grow into habits. When efficient and organized methods become second nature, they free up energy for other pursuits.

Page cards traditionally deal with communication, so the Page of Pentacles suggests that you use your ability to write letters, make phone calls, work the internet, etc., to inquire about your areas of interest, or about matters relating to a situation at hand, and share the practical knowledge gathered in your information quest.

The Page of Pentacles is focused on external realities that may at times cause him to think, "That's all there is!" He doesn't disdain the things of the spirit, they just haven't penetrated his awareness. Therefore, a reversed Page of Pentacles advises opening your awareness and cultivating an appreciation of the spiritual component of existence. You can do this by trying to appreciate the ways in which spirit can work through matter, through the things of nature.

The reversed appearance of this card may also indicate a need to let go of perfectionism and security issues, and to take some risks for the sake of learning.

Rider-Waite Tarot

Knight of Pentacles

Sacred Circle Tarot

Legend Tarot

Knight of Pentacles

The appearance of the Knight of Pentacles in an advice reading urges you to gain practical, worldly experience by taking your education, skills, and values out into the world and applying them to the problems of day-to-day living. The appearance of this card can also relate to phases in life where concentration, hard work, and goal-oriented behavior are appropriate, so it recommends accepting the work that comes your way and the obligations that are put upon you. Deal with the situation in question by formulating long-term goals: make provisions for your future security and condition yourself to work for delayed rewards.

The Knight's mode is one of service; it's important for him to have something to do, to be of use. He is a producer, a builder, a doer. He is committed to working for positive change and wants to make the world a better place. However, he is conservative in his approach because he knows that to be effective, change must often come in increments that can be integrated and solidified. You can emulate him by being patient and conscientious in assuming responsibilities. Be willing to take orders and carry out directions. Demonstrate your competence by aiming for precision and tending to details.

As a card of general advice, the Knight of Pentacles says, "Yes, now is the time to go ahead with your plan or make a commitment," especially if it involves holding responsible positions or managing money and material goods. However, proceed slowly and cautiously to minimize risk. When in doubt, it's better to err on the side of being too conservative. If you have approached the Tarot about choosing between jobs or making some other major life decision, this card advises you to choose in favor of the options that offer structure and security. If you are wondering where to go with a relationship, the Knight of Pentacles recommends commitment.

Knights show movement toward or away from something, so notice whether there is a neighboring card toward which the Knight of Pentacles is facing (various decks portray him differently). This card may indicate the nature of a responsibility that you are advised to assume.

The appearance of the Knight of Pentacles in an advice reading may also suggest that you work alongside someone who is already taking on responsibilities and can show you how to work within an organization. It especially recommends finding mentors among your fellow workers.

A reversed Knight of Pentacles might indicate that your focus is too narrow on the matter at hand and you need to create an objective distance so you can see the big picture. Try to develop greater breadth of vision by bringing in the clarity of the

Knight of Swords and the inspiration of the Knight of Wands. Experiment with imaginative problem-solving techniques. The reversed card may also suggest that although you should continue to analyze the situation in question, you should not overcommit yourself at this time, but prepare to adapt to changes in your plan.

Queen
of
Pentacles

Rider-Waite Tarot

Legend Tarot

Celtic Dragon Tarot

Queen of Pentacles

When the Queen of Pentacles is drawn in a reading for advice, the Tarot suggests that you take on a role of responsibility and look after the well-being of others, especially in matters related to material needs, personal comfort, and the physical details of life. Model the Queen of Pentacles' traits, which are characterized by constancy. This type of person is always present, consistent, devoted, and faithful in her affections and in her actions. She is also practical-minded, serious, and cautious, though she is sensual and likes to surround herself with things of quality and beauty. This card advises sharing wisdom and offering guidance, especially in practical matters involving the management of day-to-day affairs at home and at work.

Queens have a strong drive to nurture, and this is especially true of the Queen of Pentacles, whose connection to the Earth element makes her a provider of security, shelter, food, substance, and care. She is concerned with material things because they contribute to comfort and security. She relates to the Empress card as a dispenser of earthly abundance. In an advice reading, this card suggests dealing with a situation by embodying that abundance. A caretaker response may be especially applicable to questions about improving relationships. The Queen of Pentacles is very concerned about home and work environments because she recognizes how important our surroundings are to health and wholeness. You can follow her example by improving your own space with beauty and material comfort, and doing what you can to bring these qualities into your office or other work area as well.

In keeping with the Queen of Pentacles' orientation to service, you can expand your sphere of influence and become more of a power in the world through community leadership and service. Investigate existing neighborhood organizations, or larger institutions that can serve your own interests, and find ways to offer practical support and guidance; work through these conventional social forms in the mode of a nurturing Earth Mother. Traditional holiday celebrations and community festivals also provide opportunities for you to exercise the Queen of Pentacles' qualities.

To model this Queen's behavior, it may help to think of people you know of, often very maternal people, who use their personal power, aligned with traditional institutions and values, to serve family and community. The appearance of the Queen of Pentacles also suggests that you seek assistance from someone who has the resources to help you with the matter in question. Patronage is one of the Queen of Pentacles' primary blessings.

A problem the Queen of Pentacles often faces is getting bogged down in matter. Servitude to both people and the things in your life can cause you to lose touch with your intellectual and spiritual ideals. If you draw the reversed Queen of Pentacles in an advice reading, consider whether this may be the case. If so, the Tarot is urging you to unload some of your responsibilities. You can maintain the Queen of Pentacles' interests in nurturing by remembering the importance of self-nurturing: allow yourself time for essential mental and spiritual stimulation.

Earth needs moisture to be truly fruitful, so the appearance of this card reversed may suggest a need to enliven the drier, more serious, side of the Queen of Pentacles' personality with some Queen of Cups sentimentality and openness.

Rider-Waite Tarot

King
of
Pentacles

Sacred Circle Tarot

Legend Tarot

Minor Arcana: Pentacles 129

King of Pentacles

When you draw the King of Pentacles in an advice reading, the Tarot suggests that you assume a role of responsible and pragmatic leadership in order to expand your sphere of influence and deal with the situation at hand. You are especially encouraged to oversee situations involving the management and care of money, material goods and property, businesses, bureaucracies and institutions, and charitable giving.

You can best achieve this by emulating the King of Pentacles, who carries out the responsibilities of leadership in a very purposeful, conscientious, and systematic manner. He has a stabilizing effect on the people around him, and maintains order by seeing that policies and regulations are upheld. He thinks in terms of the value to be gotten out of any product, process, or enterprise. The King of Pentacles likes to work through established orders and structures, and he is usually backed by strong government, corporate, or other social and cultural authorities. Emulate him by implementing systems for greater organization and efficiency.

The King of Pentacles blesses by being a provider. He is typically a person of substance, and in an advice reading, this indicates that you should put your own resources to good use. Thus, this would be a good time to make investments and attend to business matters. If you are considering whether or not to help someone in need, this card advises you to go ahead—be generous in giving assistance and guidance—but do so in a way that you can monitor and put conditions on your support in order to assure that it is being used wisely and effectively. To model the King of Pentacles' qualities, it may help to think of people you know of, often capable managerial types, whose sense of service encourages them to help other people meet the demands and challenges of day-to-day life and work. The appearance of this card also suggests that you seek help from someone who possesses such qualities. These people have a great store of accumulated knowledge, and they are happy to dispense practical advice, often passing along some marketable skills. A King of Pentacles person can also be approached for material aid, but is most willing to give help if you have demonstrated worthiness, and if there are practical advantages to be gained.

Reversed, this card advises softening rigid behavior patterns. You can honor your King of Pentacles values and sense of duty while being less bureaucratic and more willing to accommodate new ideas. Take some risks and break some rules. Although the Pentacles court cards are earth-oriented, tend to be sensual, and enjoy good food and beautiful things, the King of Pentacles shoulders so much responsibility that he is apt to lose touch with this side of himself. If this is the case with you, it would be good to take some time off and reacquaint yourself with earthy pleasures.

Minor Arcana
Wands

Ace
of
Wands

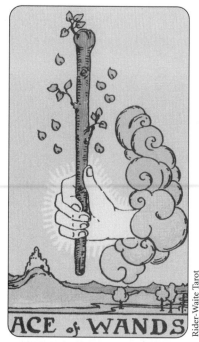

Rider-Waite Tarot

THE ACE OF WANDS

Witches Tarot

Sacred Circle Tarot

Ace of Wands

When you get the Ace of Wands in an advice reading, it is a call to action. It urges acts of power. The Ace of Wands gives the go-ahead to seize opportunities and become involved in new projects, ventures, and experiences of all sorts. Plans and programs for personal growth and advancement are especially encouraged here. Generally, in response to most questions, the Ace of Wands gives an enthusiastic "yes!" It combines the intuition that tells you to start some initiative or enterprise with the industry, effort, and driving force that enables you to make things happen. So if you have been wondering whether to act on an idea or inspiration you have had, this card says, "Yes, take the idea and run with it!" Plan to put a lot of energy into your project and keep your vision in front of you, where it will carry you into the future. Although the Aces usually signal the conception of new drives and goals, the Ace of Wands also encourages you to apply renewed inspiration and dedication to an existing project, enterprise, or goal.

Your call to action requires that you first make a decision, then commit yourself. This may take courage and resolve, but remember that this itself is an act of power. Making and committing to a decision stirs movement in the ethereal realms. This card also tells you that it's up to you alone to initiate the necessary action in the matter in question. There is some urgency here. Don't wait for others to start, and don't wait for something to "happen." Get going.

To help utilize the Ace of Wands' burst of productive energy, focus on the most direct path to completion of your goal. Act quickly. Figure out what you need to do to bring your plan to completion, then do it with dispatch. You can also get into the Ace of Wands' mode of action by recalling how you've felt on occasions when you were at your most active and enthusiastic, or by thinking about the most energetic people you know and emulating their modes of action, including their expressions, attitudes, body language, movement, etc. To help commit yourself to this new challenge, deed, enterprise, or undertaking, announce your plans to friends and family. Sometimes announcing an intention can help you carry it through, partly because the spoken word carries magical power, and partly because you may be more motivated when you want to meet other peoples' expectations.

Wands are socially oriented cards, so this card favors relationships of all sorts and advises you to use the Ace's energy to initiate social contacts. This is something that many people find extremely difficult to do. However, the people you approach will be pleased by the attention, even if they seem shy. Resist the temptation to talk about all of *your* interests; instead, ask friendly questions about *them*. This advice applies especially to young men who are afraid to approach girls. Most people will open up quite readily when encouraged to talk about themselves, and by practicing this approach, you will find it increasingly easier to strike up conversations.

If you've been thinking about starting a new venture or project and you draw the Ace of Wands reversed, this card suggests that the timing is not the best for an all-out effort. Start out more cautiously and conserve your energy. Phase into this new experience slowly. Don't worry about missing out on a great opportunity—if it's right for you, it will still be there.

Rider-Waite Tarot

Two of Wands

Legend Tarot

Celtic Dragon Tarot

Two of Wands

When the Two of Wands comes up in an advice reading, there is an indication that there are at least two viable options or courses of action open to you. To deal with this situation, you can choose one of your alternatives, or find a way to make both options work. This is a case where there is no right or wrong choice—it's almost a coin toss—but whichever path, or paths, you choose, you should commit whole-heartedly and with no regrets.

In a traditional Tarot reading, the Two of Wands can indicate that some opposition has arisen to challenge your plans or actions, and now decisions, modifications, and accommodations have to be made. However, to apply this card as advice, you might set up your own challenges. These challenges can help you set goals, define issues, and work out creative compromises. You could work out at least two alternative plans, then critique them and consider the respective pros and cons in order to decide your course of action. After you weigh the alternatives, make a choice and carry through with it. There is often a feeling of release and relief because you know that even if you aren't psychic enough to make the best possible decision, you *have* made a good decision, the most informed decision you could have made. If you want extra help in making a decision, look at any cards that flank the Two of Wands. In some decks, the man pictured faces toward one staff and away from the other. The card closest to the favored wand may give some hints about a more preferred option.

The Two of Wands, being a Wands card, deals with work, enterprise, and activity—but as a Two card, it also calls for balance in such things. If you have consulted the Tarot to ask for advice about attaining a more satisfying lifestyle, the cards may be suggesting that you find a way to achieve a more creative balance in the nature of your work and other activities. For example, consider the problem of daily work: due to the nature of the work many of us must do, we are perpetually either over-stimulated or understimulated. Many jobs require doing the same things all day long, whether it involves standing in an assembly line or behind a counter, staring at a computer screen or answering a phone with calls coming in every sixty seconds. The human body, mind, and spirit have not evolved for this type of continuous activity. If you look at hunting and gathering people, or early agriculturalists, you see that there was much day-to-day and hour-to-hour variety in their work activities. Stressfully repetitious work is a fairly modern innovation, and the need many of us have for stimulants or relaxants results from forcing ourselves to conform to unnatural demands on us. So, think about how you can arrange your activities differently, or otherwise reengineer your personal situation. You might find out whether your company will allow you to take on an added function that will be either more challenging or more relaxing, as necessary. If that isn't doable, consider having two part-time jobs rather than a full-time job that is debilitating. It might be very healthful to have two jobs with contrasting demands: one exercising your mind and the other your body.

Another possible path to wholeness is to lead a dual life. This sounds paradoxical, but many people find energy and renewal in maintaining an absorbing interest or hobby that allows them to express a totally different personality than the one they display at work. Yet another possibility is to have a job that supports your hobby, or a hobby that nicely dovetails with your work.

The Two of Wands' advice may be applied to other conditions: situations where you have to collaborate with people, or where certain types of problems have arisen. The Twos often deal with our relationships with others, so this card favors business partnerships, especially when partners complement each other's strengths and weaknesses. With larger group situations, try to get different factors or factions to work together in harmony so the projects or plans can go forward with new creative inspiration and impetus. Be flexible enough to receive input from others. Don't become addicted to your own ideas or way of doing things. When conflicting ideas and energies come into play, treat it as a stimulating game of give and take. Be willing to give and receive feedback, and modify your plans as necessary. Even if your project hasn't met with contention or opposition, it might be wise to pause, perhaps at the halfway point, assess your progress, look at pros and cons in the current plan, and consider whether there are any special factors that need modification or accommodation.

When the Two of Wands comes up reversed in an advice reading, you may be urged to separate and put more distance between at least two different factors in your work, home life, or other personal affairs. Give them equal consideration, but study or develop them in isolation from each other. Where people are involved, give both sides an equal hearing, then try to provide each with separate spheres of influence. You may also be in a unique situation where it is in your best interest to keep different facets of your life in separate compartments, perhaps even maintaining dual identities. Because you are reading a book on Tarot, you have some interest in occult matters, which is something a large segment of our society disapproves of. Perhaps there is a need to keep this, or another personal matter, secret from neighbors or coworkers who might be spooked by your interests, however innocent.

Three
of
Wands

Three of Wands

When the Three of Wands comes up in an advice reading, the Tarot is telling you that in order to solve problems creatively, and make things happen in your life, you must take your plans, efforts, talents, and creative resources out into the world.

The best place to start is in your immediate community. You may first need to identify the environment, place, or people that you consider to be your community. Think of ways you can put your energy and know-how to work in your community, especially in cooperation with groups of people (as in service clubs or other community projects), and make your efforts known. Get out and around, and explore your environment. Even in your own neighborhood there may be unique and interesting businesses, services, and other places that you have not previously noticed. Make a point of learning what's going on around you. Get to know what community resources can help you attain your goals—as well as the ways in which you can be a resource to your community.

The Waite deck's illustration of the Three of Wands card shows no additional human figures beside a man looking out to sea, but the combination of the socially oriented Wands cards with the family- and community-oriented number Three makes interactions with other people an important theme of this card. Social interactions are especially important in promoting the synthesis of ideas that produces new creative products, inventions, and enterprises, which are also concerns of the Three of Wands. This card is associated with trade and commerce, moreso from an interest in the way new products influence lifestyles, ideas, and culture change than in the acquisition and exchange of material goods.

Communication networks and travel are also important in linking communities and exchanging ideas. You may be able to apply these things to your own situation by writing and conversing, gathering and circulating information, networking, and attending meetings, workshops, seminars, and other events where you can be exposed to lots of new things and interact with a wide variety of people. The quality of stimulation you will experience will spark creative solutions to some of the problems you may be experiencing.

The Three of Wands is also a rather future-oriented card, concerned with invention and "the coming thing." It recommends that you look outward, make plans for the future, and direct your energy outward by reaching for, and seizing, more opportunities. You could say that this is a card about setting your ship out to sail. To expand your horizons, you should also broaden your range of interests, investigate new things, and follow where your curiosity leads you.

Generally, the Three of Wands advises in favor of business and enterprises of all sorts, especially those involving commerce and the exchange of ideas. If you are wondering whether to go along with a coming trend or some other futuristic venture, this card is for it. This card also suggests involvement in learning and teaching situations, interacting with committees and other cooperative projects, networking, and all forms of communication as means for dealing with the matter in question. However, this card does not recommend getting into one-on-one relationships or other sorts of single-focused commitments. It favors playing the field and keeping your options open.

If the Three of Wands comes up reversed in an advice reading, the orientation to trade, travel, idea exchange, and community action is still present, but a narrower focus is suggested. Perhaps you should pull back a bit, conserve some energy, limit your sphere of activity and influence, and concentrate on a smaller area of endeavor. Adventures and forays into the wider world should be undertaken with the understanding and intent to go forth, but then return, bringing something back to your home and inner life.

four of Wands

WANDS (4) WANDS

Perfected Work

four of Wands

The Four of Wands can represent a rest from, a reward for, and a formal recognition of, effort, enterprise, and accomplishment. It illustrates the desire to enjoy the fruits of labor, and to celebrate achievement with ceremony, or with things that are lasting and tangible.

As a card of advice, the Four of Wands suggests that you lay plans and foundations, work for solid goals and objectives, and honor and celebrate your relationships and your achievements. If you are consulting the Tarot for advice on major decisions, this card suggests that you choose in favor of those options that will provide a solid base from which to build upward, enabling you to put down roots and enjoy order and stability.

Illustrations of the Four of Wands often imply a ceremonial occasion or ritual space because human nature likes to seek public recognition for individual accomplishments, attainment of position, and committed relationships. Thus, the Four of Wands advises you to act on your plans and give them material expression. In work or business, you may do something to make your own position official, formalize partnerships, establish an office or workplace if you have not already done so, consolidate your holdings, and launch public relations campaigns that will enhance your company's place in the community. In relationships, this may suggest proposing marriage, and/or the establishment of a household. On a personal level, plan special ways to commemorate your life's milestones and landmarks. Honor and acknowledge events and occasions meaningful to those around you with gifts, cards, and words of congratulations, and by accepting invitations to weddings, graduations, and so on.

As with the other Four cards, the Four of Wands can stand for house and home. For many people, having a dream house, or at least a home base, is something that inspires them to work, strive, and save, and is often a key component of "the American dream." In return, the home accommodates many physical and psychological needs. A house can provide material security (represented by the Four of Pentacles), emotional comfort (the Four of Cups), and retreat from worldly strife (the Four of Swords), but it can also support the creative and competitive needs represented by the Wands suit (and Wands people). It serves as a center for the creative life by providing a place to work on projects, as well as a place to express personal creativity and style through decoration and design. Responsible household management also confers community standing, and serves as a symbol of accomplishment. The Four of Wands suggests that you have come to an interlude, a place in life, where you should put some creative energy into house and home or other personal projects. If you are thinking of buying a home or working at home, this card is definitely in favor of it. In other applications, it urges you to claim or create a work space or some sort of base of operations.

When the Four of Wands is reversed in an advice reading, there is an indication that you desire to achieve common goals such as security, worldly position, and respectability. Maintaining the lifestyle that goes with these things may inhibit your need for action and creative expression. You can continue to maintain your goals, relationships, home base, and work space for the sake of security and stability, but it may be a good idea to find ways to take time off and get out to explore, try new things, and take some calculated risks. The reversed Four of Wands may also suggest opening up your personal space, letting in the world in a bigger or more significant way, or by promoting a more casual atmosphere in your workplace. Uphold ceremonies and traditions that affirm important values, but soften your insistence on position or formality if there are boundaries between yourself and other people.

five
of
Wands

FIVE

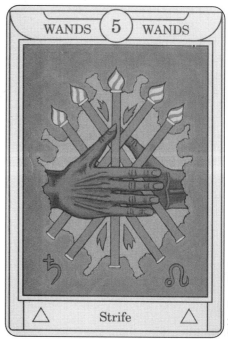

WANDS 5 WANDS

Strife

five of Wands

The Five cards represent the addition of a new element to a stable system or complacent situation. This can be experienced as stimulating or stressful, depending on how you perceive and react to change. In the case of the Five of Wands, this element of change is often sparked by competition and can affect our work efforts, our plans and goals, our interactions with larger groups of people, and our ways of doing things. The Waite deck's illustration portrays a group of men contending with each other in a melee, using the Wand symbols as quarterstaffs. Although the staffs are clashing against each other, no one seems threatened with serious injury. In line with the sporting values of the Wands suit, this card is not about violent conflict, but rather the stimulating changes and competitive challenges resulting from asserting one's energy and ego in the realm of activity, creativity, and enterprise.

As a card of advice, the Five of Wands' broadest application is to make choices in favor of change, to bring novelty and stimulation into any situation you are dealing with, and to go where the action is. It hints that the measures or actions you have been taking are not enough, and you must bring yourself up to a higher level of activity and productivity. If you have gotten too settled in the status quo, this may require you to remotivate yourself. Fortunately, there is an abundance of motivational speakers and inspirational authors, so you can get psyched up by going to workshops or reading books on how to deal with stress, change, and challenge.

Taking inspiration from the Five of Wands, exercise your personal skills by setting up your own tests and by using competition as a motivator and force for change. Compete against yourself by trying to beat your past records, and push yourself to get out and get involved in situations that take you outside of your ordinary boundaries. Take up challenges from other people in order to keep fit and competitive, even if you have to go up against other egos. The implications of this card of active and aggressive interchange may be especially meaningful to entrepreneurs, executives, people who deal with the public, and others who are in the thick of things and must be competitive to thrive. However, its advice also applies to creative folk, as competition can spur creativity. The Five of Wands denotes a strong desire for self-expression, especially as stimulated by competitive situations that enable you to improve your skills, communication, and creative powers. Therefore, take this card's advice by finding an outlet (especially in a public arena) for your creative energies. You can decide how much friendly rivalry you are willing to take on, and how you will comport yourself if your personal creative expression challenges other peoples' competitive instincts. You do not need to become involved in the most aggressive and stressful competitive activities to seek this stimulation; you can experience this card's energies through gentle and sociable sports and games. Interaction with others, even when stressful or competitive, helps you cultivate your social IQ, which is so important to success.

This Tarot card is particularly concerned with group interactions. Wands represent ideas and inspirations converted into energy and enterprise, and in order for those things to have outer-world value, they have to stand up to public challenges. That means they have to be put to the test and face the competition. As a call for action, the Five of Wands may also advocate some form of social activism. Do you feel compelled to forsake personal peace and security for a larger cause? This card urges you to get involved.

The Five of Wands' stressful aspects can also relate to the many distractions of daily life. It's an unfortunate fact of modern life that we go about our daily routines in anticipation of disruption. Perhaps the best way to adapt to this is to view the myriad interruptions and minor crises that arise as part of the necessary and wholesome rhythm and flow of life rather than regarding life as something that happens in between the disturbances.

If the Five of Wands comes up reversed, it offers advice to people with a touch of agoraphobia or social phobia, or others for whom entry into spirited competition and commotion would be too intimidating. If this is true for you, you might approach new and confusing situations more tentatively, skirting the edges, and becoming involved in smaller and more mannered group situations, especially ones that are enjoyable.

There is another type of personality for whom the reversed Five of Wands' advice might apply: do you have a tendency to go running to every conflict, to throw yourself into every debate or controversy? Or are you, perhaps, involved in activities that make too many demands on you? This card may be advising you to pull back a bit by modulating the stressful qualities of the Fives with the regenerative qualities of the Fours. Balance your slate of activities by focusing more on the domestic or settled life (as depicted in the Four of Wands or Pentacles), reevaluating your situation and its impact on your feelings (the Four of Cups), or seeking regenerative rest (as suggested in the Four of Swords). You may feel that you need to keep adding new projects to stay sharp or to keep your business competitive, but the Tarot is suggesting that you can get along fine at a slower pace.

Rider-Waite Tarot

Six
of
Wands

Witches Tarot

SIX

SIX OF SPEARS

THE RETURN
OF AMBROSIUS

Legend Tarot

Six of Wands

The Six of Wands relates to the experience of riding high and feeling confident in yourself because you know that you can handle challenges competently and resourcefully. It represents a peaceful and productive state of affairs that you have made possible through energetic dedication to your goals. There is an implication that you have already triumphed over some very challenging situations. Now you have proven yourself, to yourself as well as to others, and have a right to enjoy some of the privileges of your position.

As an advice card, the Six of Wands recommends that you focus on an important goal, and summon and direct your productive energies into this objective. This card especially favors involvement in projects, activities, and enterprises as an expression of your skill and competence. Do things right, maintain order, and improve your systems so your efforts will pay off. When systems are set up properly, things will go more smoothly; when the machinery has been set in motion, it will carry you forward, and success and victory are assured. You can stretch the Six of Wands state of flow, and your own feelings of peak performance, by rewarding yourself for your accomplishments. If you don't have any great goals or noble purposes to accomplish, then turn your mind to the affairs of daily life. If you can do the work before you skillfully and efficiently, you can count that as a minor triumph and give yourself little rewards for getting things done.

The Six of Wands also advises you to maintain a winning mindset: one of optimism, expansiveness, and the belief that you are able to stay on top of all situations. Success is a natural consequence of being willing and able to take on challenges, so deal with delays, obstacles, and other problems by viewing them as part of life's parade, rather than as roadblocks on your path. A positive attitude is especially necessary to success in your daily work life. If you feel that your work is unrewarding, adjust your attitude so that you view the efforts you expend as your service to the universe, no matter how humble your job. The Six of Wands' attitude calls for magnanimity of character—be generous with your time and understanding, and stay above all niggling worries and petty conflicts. This card has affinities with the planet Jupiter in Leo, a sign of power and leadership because of its style and magnanimity.

If you're down in the dumps and see no way of applying the Six of Wands' mode of thought to your present condition, search your memory for past times and events when you did enjoy the sensation of top performance, when you really shined and triumphed over challenges. Find ways to recreate those activities and experiences. Also, the Six of Wands can pertain to time set aside for creative work, and for moments of creative living, so improve your situation by looking for ways to bring creative activity and ambience into your daily routine.

When reversed, the Six of Wands may suggest a need to rein in your energy and enthusiasm. If you are getting involved in some new enterprise, or trying to accomplish a seemingly immense purpose, this reversed card urges you not to overreach yourself. Instead, it might be wise to go after your objective by planning a series of smaller steps that present more easily manageable challenges.

Seven of Wands

Rider-Waite Tarot

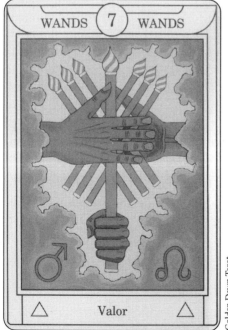

Golden Dawn Tarot

Celtic Dragon Tarot

Seven of Wands

The type of challenges that are denoted by the Seven of Wands test your personal ingenuity and your belief in yourself. Wands represent inspiration and energy, and Sevens stand for vision and experimentation, so this card often pertains to people with unique ideas, or those who have personal visions they are trying to put into practice. As a card of general advice, the Seven of Wands promotes individualism and the expression and assertion of difference. It encourages you to develop and affirm your ego identity and to go after your desires and stand up for your beliefs. If you believe you should get involved or take action on a matter, you must do so, even if others do not see the need and are not in accord. There is a saying that asking for forgiveness is easier than asking for permission.

The Seven of Wands' vision and inventiveness suggest solving problems and finding better ways to do things. Let this inspire you to take an idea and improve it, and to show its viability in other applications. The mode of enterprising energy and idea orientation involved here can give you the impetus to take some chances. However, in order to take risks, you must have conviction and an ability to see opportunities that others cannot see, based on a genuine knowledge of the elements involved.

Innovators often have a lonely struggle, and the popular illustration of the Seven of Wands, which shows a man standing his ground while using his stave to fight off an onslaught, can relate to the position of the lone visionary who must rely on the strength of his or her convictions to stand up against the naysayers. To pursue your vision, you may have to go through a period of isolation, and you may have to break with convention. Perhaps it will be necessary to go against the wishes of friends, family, and community, or against your academic and professional associations. Expect to have to explain and justify yourself, and to defend your actions and ideas over and over if necessary. This struggle to assert the things that are meaningful to the individual relates to what Angeles Arrien calls "the quality of valour, . . . the courage to stand by what you value" in her analysis of the Thoth deck in *The Tarot Handbook*, where she labels the Seven of Wands as "Valour" (p. 183). Sometimes, original thinkers have to prove themselves repeatedly, even though they've had previous successes. As advice, this card urges you to keep going, to have faith in yourself and your beliefs, to persevere. After a while, people may come to accept that however novel your ideas are, you can probably accomplish them.

Although the man commonly pictured in the illustration of the Seven of Wands is beset by opposition, he seems to be prevailing because he has positioned himself well and taken the high ground. This, too, can be interpreted as advice. If you are in an adversarial situation, be sure that you have all of the skills, information, and documentation you need to prove your position. Take the moral high ground—don't do anything to compromise your integrity. High ground always wins.

When you draw the reversed Seven of Wands in an advice reading, it could suggest either a need to give some ground, or to let go of the need to justify yourself. You may be unreasonable or inflexible perhaps in trying to push for changes that would be too unsettling for other people. Although your plans and ideas are basically good, you could use some input from other people, and you should take their security needs and their feelings into consideration. At the same time, getting feedback from considerate and intelligent people can offset the sort of exaggerated criticism you may be getting from the anonymous but critical audience we sometimes construct in our minds,* and against whom we waste time mentally defending ourselves. The reversed card may also suggest giving up a position of advantage in favor of maintaining harmony.

* Writing guru Peter Elbow points out that this "dangerous audience" in the mind is often responsible for stultifying would-be writers and others (*Writing With Power*, pp. 186–87).

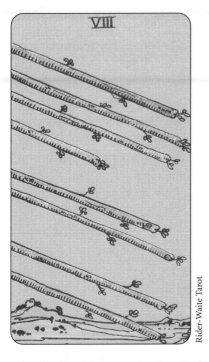

Eight of Wands

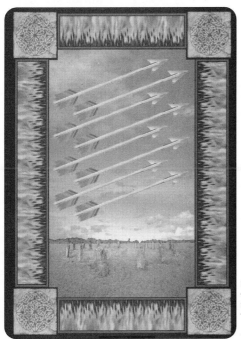

Minor Arcana: Wands   153

Eight of Wands

Eights represent planning and organization, and Wands relate to ideas, enthusiasm, and creative will, so the Eight of Wands shows the purposeful direction of energy toward a projected outcome. It indicates that things are falling into place, that diverse energies are working together toward the completion of a goal. These ideas are indicated in the popular pictorial representation of this card: a tight group of eight rods or arrows directed toward a destination.

In an advice reading, this card can be readily and generally interpreted: gather your energies and resources, then focus them on the object of your desires. The Eight of Wands may be suggesting that the timing is right to put things into action and proceed quickly, but in an orderly and deliberate manner, to assure that your plans and projects unfold as they should. Think about how your actions will affect the sequence of events leading into the future so that you will be prepared for all contingencies. Pull all of the parts together, attending to the details and tying up loose ends. Work toward harmony among coworkers, family members, or others— and treat each individual's contribution as equally important, in line with the unity of purpose suggested by the Eight of Wands. A successful conclusion cannot then be far away.

In line with other traditional interpretations of this card, the Eight of Wands advises that this is a good time to travel and send messages.

The Eight of Wands may also apply to social trends and historical forces, indicating that a lot of people, things, or events are moving in the same direction, and that momentum is building. As an advice card, this might suggest that it is a good time to identify such trends and try to take advantage of them, or move with them, finding ways to let their energies carry you along into the future. This may have special meaning for entrepreneurs, designers, writers, politicians, and others who need to know which way the energy is moving. If you're thinking of investing your time or money in a futuristic project, this card is in favor of it.

If you draw the Eight of Wands reversed, this may suggest that you should slow the pace of a project or enterprise you are working on, perhaps to prevent its parts or elements from being pulled together too sloppily or hastily. It might be a good idea to review all stages of your plan. If you have set an arbitrary deadline, think about giving yourself an extension. Don't try to force matters or speed things up; all is not yet ready. Use your time to look into details. Go back over your notes and plans to see if there is research to be done or paperwork to be gathered, people to be contacted, or other little details that need to be taken care of before things can fall into place. Make sure that all of the people involved are in accord and ready to move in the same direction.

An alternate interpretation for the reversed card suggests that perhaps things are headed for an outcome that will not be beneficial, so it would be better to interrupt the proceedings or direct your energies elsewhere. If this card is part of a layout, the card or portion of a card that the reversed wands are pointing to may suggest the best place for personal efforts to be redirected. The reversed card may also hint that you can achieve success by going with a "retro" movement.

Nine
of
Wands

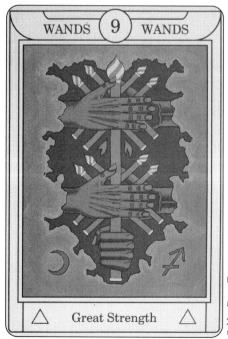

Great Strength

Nine of Wands

The Nine of Wands represents the need to deal with a proliferation of energies as you participate in the world of ideas and enterprise. It puts your personal competence and convictions to the test, which may be why Arthur Edward Waite says in *The Pictorial Key to the Tarot* that this card "signifies strength in opposition" (p. 180), and the Thoth deck simply labels it "Strength." Pictorial versions of this card, which portray a man who shoulders a quarterstaff and stands warily before a picket of staves, emphasize the theme of strength in defense. The self-replicating number nine intensifies the active qualities of the Wands, attracting more activities to you and calling for the vitality to match them. Some interpreters link this card astrologically with the Sun and Moon in Sagittarius, which are also concerned with a high degree of physical and mental activity, as well as the expression of beliefs.

As a card of general advice, the Nine of Wands urges you to exercise your personal strength in any matter in question, especially in the expression of your convictions. You may find yourself in the position of having to defend your beliefs and independent ways of doing things. You may find yourself taking on a lot of responsibilities as a way of demonstrating your personal potency. Don't allow others to push you to make decisions, or to get into things you feel uneasy about or unready for. Be aware of your vulnerabilities; because the Wands tend to pertain to activities and enterprises, your vulnerabilities may stem from problems with your own performance. Try to arrange matters so that you can accentuate your strong points and minimize your weak points. Don't take on positions or projects that would strain your abilities. Call on the energetic, inspirational nature of the Wands suit to boost your confidence.

As an extension of the idea of defense, you might take various practical measures for your protection, such as improving your personal and home security. In professional and legal matters, make sure that all of your ideas and assertions are well supported and documented.

The Nine cards also have a lot to do with lifestyles, so this card tends to represent a situation in which multiple activities are a way of life. If you wish to emulate this style, be optimistic, act from the competitive side of your nature, enlarge your range of expectations, and work at generating the vitality you'll need to keep different projects going. Take advantage of all the opportunities that arise. You will be able to enjoy peak experiences as you pull ideas and activities together, and plan new ones with a sense of mission or purpose. If you feel expansive, this is a good time to make improvements, implement multiple projects, and expand your business.

In an advice reading, the reversed Nine of Wands may caution against taking on so many activities that you become frustrated, cannot focus well on any one project, and become alienated from your relationships. Start simplifying your life by being more selective about what you get involved in.

The reversed Nine of Wands may also advise you not to be too opinionated, suggesting that you give up the need to be right. Be willing to give weight to other peoples' beliefs, and to try new ways of doing things. Allow yourself to be more vulnerable, as you must let your guard down in order to achieve intimacy with others. Try not to be too sensitive: do not react to disagreement as a personal attack or a sign of rejection. There may also be a need for you to try to understand and evaluate how your actions and accomplishments express your belief systems. Where have they brought you? Where do you still need to go?

Ten
of
Wands

Ten of Wands

The Ten of Wands, which commonly depicts a man carrying a heavy load of staves toward a special destination, shows us how we can draw on our accumulation of achievements, know-how, and insights, to work toward our goals. The situation here is one that requires your full commitment and the sense of a greater mission or purpose. The nature of the work in question, though often applied to career goals, is probably integral to your path in life.

The Ten of Wands may come up when you're concerned about making your mark in the world and are building for the future, striving for something that will bring you wider recognition or fulfill a sense of mission. This card advises you to assess your experiences in order to decide what you want to take with you as you either continue or set forth on your rightful path. It urges you to persevere. If you can try to understand how the tasks you've undertaken support your life's purpose, it will be easier to carry on. Some lines from *I Ching for Beginners* by Kristyna Arcati share the Ten of Wands' concern with tasks and cycles, "By persevering does he complete things in their due time. Each end is a new beginning" (p. 26). The Ten of Wands' concern with cycles also lets you know that it is never too late to start working on a meaningful goal—or to start over. Opportunities come around again and again, though of course, you have to be willing to go out to meet them.

As a card of general advice, the Ten of Wands may indicate that you should take on some responsibilities, perhaps even multiple responsibilities, in order to fulfill your obligations to family and society, or to work toward a special goal. Your personal competence and conscientiousness may well attract extra work and responsibilities to you, but this is just something you must learn to accept. The positive side is that you gain recognition for your accomplishments and seldom have to worry about being out of work. Where projects are concerned, take all elements into account. You may have to manage all phases of a project. If the work seems oppressive to you (like some sort of indentureship), you may have to summon all of your energy and strength, but there is an indication that the job is not greater than you can bear, and that rest and relief are not far off.

Viewed from another perspective, the man shown in the popular pictorial versions of the Ten of Wands may be seen as strong rather than overburdened. Regarding relationships with family, friends, coworkers, and others, you may have to allow yourself to be imposed on. You may even have to carry certain people who need your help, or who won't assume their share of responsibilities, in order to complete your task.

A possible alternative interpretation for advice may be extrapolated from an element of the card's pictorial symbolism: the traditional symbol of the bundled sticks asserts that in union there is strength. Here, the card calls for collective action. Consider bringing your friends, family, or other associates together to get a job done, or to unite for some other important purpose.

When you draw the Ten of Wands reversed, it may suggest a need to draw some personal boundaries to limit the amount of responsibility you are willing to take on. ("I will do this and this, but not that.") Evaluate which of your burdens serve personal goals, and which have been imposed by family and society. Successful perseverance and the motivational nature of the Wands cards favor inner-directed objectives. It may help to put yourself in a different mode of thought, where you're not constantly trying to calculate what you'll get out of a job and how soon it will be over. Rather, focus on the basic dignity and self-worth inherent in working hard to maintain or accomplish something. While maintaining responsibility for your project, try to delegate or contract some of the work.

The reversed Ten of Wands may also indicate a need to backtrack. A project may need to be reorganized or reworked, or you may come to the recognition that your entire life's work needs to take a new direction or start new. If so, take heart from the words of Kipling, who reminds us that,

> If you can force your heart and nerve and sinew
> To serve your turn long after they are gone,
> And so hold on when there is nothing in you
> Except the Will which says to them: Hold on!

then you can also

> Watch the things you gave your life to, broken,
> And stoop and build 'em up with worn-out tools. (*If*, p. 133)

which is one of the marks of the full maturity called for by the Ten of Wands.

Page
of
Wands

Rider-Waite Tarot

THE PRINCESS OF WANDS

Witches Tarot

Celtic Dragon Tarot

Page of Wands

Page cards relate to the roles and faces we try on in our ongoing learning process, as part of the lifelong work of establishing identity. When the Page of Wands comes up in an advice reading, the Tarot indicates that this is a time to become involved in learning experiences that promote identity growth—especially those experiences that allow us to develop creative ideas and to assert them in the social world.

The Page of Wands is a person who is learning to make his way in the world. This Page wants to be where the action is, and is learning the ropes, studying the networks of activity and enterprise. The Page of Wands is also eager to communicate his lessons and ideas, but at this stage, has more enthusiasm than experience. However, this character does have creative will: when the Page of Wands perceives that something needs to be done, he will get right on it, often tackling the situation in a bold and innovative manner.

This card advises learning in a very active manner, by getting out and doing, so say "yes" to new experiences. If you are considering some sort of internship, you should accept it. Another good way for Page of Wands types to become involved in the action and activities they seek is to join clubs for people with special interests. Service clubs also provide opportunities for real-world experience. This card may suggest finding a fellow learner with a high level of energy and enthusiasm with whom to share projects and adventures. You can stimulate each other's interests and cheer each other on.

It is a fact that one of the best ways to learn a subject is to teach it, and any teacher will relate experiences of having to stay one or two steps ahead of the students—learning and teaching at the same time. In order to show someone else how to do something, you must first be sure that you thoroughly understand it yourself, and then (which is more difficult) you must be able to articulate it, explain it clearly and concisely. This means of learning relates to the Page of Wands' function as a card of communications. As practical advice, find something that interests you, start learning it, and share your experiences with others as you go along. Choose in favor of careers and other options that involve teaching and communicating. In relationships, it's important that you be able to communicate "where you're at."

The Page of Wands advises you to speak up and speak out if there is something you are concerned about. Learners, who are often in a dependent and disempowered state, may feel that they don't have a right to say anything. However, to learn, you must ask questions, and to develop identity, you must be able to try out your own words. The Page of Wands is very much a card about finding your own voice.

However, the reversed Page of Wands may denote a need to withhold information. Sometimes you can shoot yourself in the foot by revealing too much about yourself. For example, experts on job interviewing advise: don't let a prospective employer lead you into reciting your entire life history; keep the conversation relevant to the skills required for the job. Most people, if allowed to talk too long, will reveal things that detract from the image of confidence and competence one needs to put forth. Thus, the Tarot may be saying, "Don't pass up an opportunity to keep your mouth shut."*

The Page of Wands is eager to get in on the action, but as a learner, he needs to cultivate patience. If this card comes up reversed, it may suggest that although your ideas and inspirations are good, they require further development. More practical and social experience will add depth and viability to your plans and visions.

* A favorite saying of my dad's.

Rider-Waite Tarot

Knight
of
Wands

Witches Tarot

Sacred Circle Tarot

Knight of Wands

When the Knight of Wands comes up in an advice reading, you are called to put your ideas to the test by taking them out into real-world situations and applications. This card gives the go-ahead on getting involved in new projects and enterprises, and experiences of all sorts.

Energy and enthusiasm are outstanding Knight of Wands characteristics. In fact, this Knight's desire to express his energy and potency may be more important to him than the causes he takes up or the things he actually achieves as a result. You will find him where the action is. In fact, he has an uncanny ability to sense in advance where the action is going to be. He is always moving forward, taking things as they come, while working on his own progress and self-development.

It is a Knight's job to tackle problems, and sometimes the Knight of Wands has to deal with projects and enterprises that seem to be faltering. However, nothing stimulates this Knight like a challenge, so it is under just such circumstances that he enjoys peak performance and his greatest creativity. If you have been encountering setbacks in your own affairs, model this energetic, competitive mode of thinking.

Knights can show movement toward or away from a matter, so examine adjacent cards toward which the Knight of Wands is going (he is portrayed differently in different decks), as this may signal a special opportunity to take advantage of.

When you draw the Knight of Wands, the Tarot may also advise you to seek out a person with similar talents and goals because the stimulation of shared activities will propel you both forward. The Knight of Wands can be a friend whose enthusiasm pulls you into the thick of things, into outer-world adventures that force you to apply effort and intelligence to new and challenging enterprises.

Like all of the Wands court, this Knight is an idea person. However, he must beware of falling in love with his own ideas. Not all ideas are workable or marketable, so an idea person has to be objective enough to discard the ones that won't have a reasonable payoff, in the knowledge that there will always be another brainstorm coming along. If this card comes up reversed in an advice reading, it may denote a need to let go of an idea or project, and go back to the drawing board to develop the more promising ones. Wands types are so enthused with their own ideas that they may also be intolerant or unwilling to consider the ideas of others, so the reversed appearance of this card urges you to respect other peoples' need to shine. Try not to cut them out or upstage them.

The reversed Knight of Wands may also warn you not to take on new projects or activities. You are eager to get started, but you are advised to rein in your enthusiasm so your energies don't get so scattered that you become ineffective. Perhaps you are already overprogrammed, or perhaps the Tarot foresees even busier times ahead. Pulling back will give you a pause to make sure that your energies are focused on the right objectives. In a regular reading, a reversed Knight of Wands may denote someone who has slanted *chi* (a disrupted flow of life energy); because his work and other efforts are not aligned with his heart's desires, energy is diverted into daydreams, projects that don't go anywhere, and other wasted efforts.

Queen
of
Wands

Queen of Wands

If the Queen of Wands comes up in an advice reading, the Tarot suggests that you assert your personal power to go after your desires. You can best achieve this by adopting the Queen of Wands' active mind, personal passion, competence, self-assurance, and ability to act on feelings. Wands cards have intuitive qualities, and with the Queen, these powers are especially strong. Therefore, this card advises you to trust and act on your instincts. Follow your intuition in pursuing a career or other absorbing interest that allows you full expression of your creative will.

Focus attention on your personal growth and advancement, as self-interest and self-improvement are major motivating factors for the Wands Queen. As a card of advice, the Queen of Wands has special meaning for those seeking encouragement to get off welfare or out of other debilitating lifestyles. The welfare lifestyle, which is guaranteed to send anyone on a nosedive into depression, is antithetical to the Queen of Wands' proactive way of doing things. Queens are doers. To climb out of the abyss, summon all of your energy to act as if you are the Queen of Wands, even though such a high-energy personality may initially be hard to sustain. People think that our moods determine our behavior, but science has discovered that it also works the other way around: our behavior can alter our moods. Put yourself through the physical motions that an optimistic, energetic, self-confident person would display, and optimism, energy, and self-confidence will follow. Adopting the Queen of Wands' persona can also help you overcome abuse, other types of dependent relationships, and depressive, self-defeating patterns of all sorts.

If you have approached the Tarot about romantic concerns, take the initiative in seeking love and approaching the object of your desire. If you have long been single and are experiencing a corresponding loss of energy and drive, the Queen of Wands' approach to life enables you to become reacquainted with your libido. This will result in total regeneration, affecting a lot more than your love life. The Queen of Wands enjoys life fully, and her energetic nature expresses itself in sensual pleasures, recreational pursuits, social interactions, and all sorts of creative projects.

To model this Queen's exuberant style, emulate people you know of (such as celebrities or acquaintances) who use wit, charm, and a high level of energy to act on their creative urges. Utilize creative will to transform your appearance and environment, and bring flair and ingenuity into your daily work. The Queen of Wands card may also suggest that you seek out a person who understands and supports your needs for self-assertion and expression. Queen of Wands types will champion innovative people and their causes.

The Queen of Wands has a special interest in encouraging and nurturing talent, so take action to make things happen for yourself and others. Put your energy into cultivating your social affiliations, and maintain a network or a community of choice. Use your skills and resources to bring creative people, ideas, and things together. Identify capability and talent in the people around you, then promote their interests. You will find that you thereby also promote your own interests and well-being.

Because Queen of Wands people get involved in so many activities and have so many demands on their time, they are apt to become overprogrammed. The appearance of the reversed Queen of Wands card may advise cutting back on activities and finding more time for solitude. Time spent alone can enable Wands personalities to bring greater depth and insight into the ideas and ideals that come to them so naturally.

KING of WANDS

King
of
Wands

Minor Arcana: Wands 171

King of Wands

In an advice reading, court cards suggest modes of thinking and acting that you can adopt in order to deal with different situations. When you draw the King of Wands, the Tarot urges you to assume a "take charge" personality. Take the lead in projects, business, creative activities, and other enterprises while focusing on inspired goals. Emulate the King of Wands' style of leadership, which is bold, energetic, and enthusiastic. He acts quickly and decisively. He is willing to take risks, and if he makes a mistake, he knows how to get out of it. Because of his high energy and charisma, he inspires others by his own example.

The King of Wands is a good communicator and negotiator. He is highly competitive, but also principled, generous, and magnanimous. He is most likely to be in business for himself. Although he may run an aggressive business, he brings a touch of idealism into his enterprises, believing that they serve the course of human progress. His dedication and high level of competence result in many solid achievements and material rewards. He is less interested in the products of his efforts than in the challenges he tackles. He has many responsibilities related to his many accomplishments, yet he is always alert for new projects, enterprises, and opportunities. Thus, the King of Wands card advises you to be open to ideas and opportunities, and to be flexible and ready to implement changes when needed.

To model the King's personality style, it may help to think about the most energetic achievers you know, as they are likely to be King of Wands types. Adopt their can-do attitudes and modes of acting. Experiment with ways to boost your level of energy and enthusiasm, and cultivate an expansive, optimistic outlook so you can see the opportunities inherent in everything—even in larger social problems and economic setbacks. Much of the King of Wands' success stems from his ability to deal with situations as they arise, without losing energy or focus.

The appearance of the King of Wands may suggest that you seek help from people who possess his qualities when you want to launch a new project or solve a long-standing problem. Because they're so busy, these people are hard to get hold of. However, once you have their attention, they are willing to help you get started—especially with imaginative enterprises—if you show drive and enthusiasm.

When the King of Wands comes up reversed, the Tarot may be telling you that you have become too identified with this King's "type A" personality traits. Perhaps you have been scattering your energies and alienating your loved ones by trying to accomplish too many things. In order to cope, maintain your King of Wands ideals and ideas, but moderate your actions and try a more laid-back mode of behavior, such as that of the King of Cups.

Minor Arcana
Cups

Ace
of
Cups

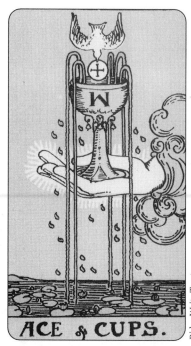
Rider-Waite Tarot

Sacred Circle Tarot

Legend Tarot

Ace of Cups

The Ace of Cups represents the richness of the emotional life, the inner life. It can represent the emergence of new feelings, along with awareness of these feelings. This card may also betoken a new beginning that you will find spiritually nourishing and emotionally regenerative. When you draw the Ace of Cups in an advice reading, you are urged to open yourself to new feelings and emotions. Enrich your personal experiences by trying to bring a deeper and more genuine level of feeling to your actions and interactions. Put more feeling into everything you do.

The Ace of Cups relates to our emotional issues, so when this card comes up in an advice reading, think about how your unconscious motivations for security and fulfillment (often rooted in childhood experience) relate to the depth and quality of your relationships, your capacity for sympathetic imagination (empathy), your desire for connection with a larger community, and the spiritual wellsprings that nurture your inner and outer lives.

To experience an influx of new feelings, it's important to learn how to manage emotions. If you have consulted the Tarot about your emotional state, the Ace of Cups advises reframing your thoughts to produce a more positive outlook. Use mood management and positive-thinking techniques to see things in a brighter light. To carry the Ace of Cups' energy forward, imagine (or if you can, reexperience) the free flow of feelings that creates rapport with other people, and with the living world around you. Visualize ebullient sensations welling up within you. Imagine what it would be like to be overflowing with joy and happiness. Model whichever facet of your personality best expresses this emotional openness, or try to emulate the ways of people you know who express well the Cups suit's deep emotional and spiritual qualities.

In line with the theme of nourishment, this card certainly advises you to nourish yourself, spiritually as well as emotionally. Seek out the kinds of experiences and things that revive your spiritual nature, that remind you that you are a spiritual being. Thomas Moore's suggestions in *Care of the Soul*, and Clarissa Pinkola Estes' comments on reclaiming the soul life in *Women Who Run with the Wolves*, relate to the profound refreshment suggested by the Ace of Cups.

In order to fully experience the rich inner life the Ace of Cups promises, it is also important to open yourself to other people. An important way to materialize the promises of the Ace of Cups card is to invite greater intimacy into your personal relationships. Here I use intimacy in the old-fashioned sense of the word, that is, shared confidences. Perhaps you are advised to deal with a situation in question by reaching out to others, even if there's some risk of hurt or rejection. This card definitely says "yes" to questions about getting involved in new relationships. As an Ace, it advises taking the initiative in approaching others and starting relationships.

To carry out this card's theme of extending nourishment, give generously of yourself. Try to generate an abundance of good feelings so there will be plenty to spread around. Give and receive blessings, which may take the form of good words, shared joys, and little favors. Offering emotional nutrition to others can also mean giving encouragement and cheer. It can mean giving help, even if that means just being there for someone. It also means giving unconditional love.

In any decision that you are currently contemplating—whether it be related to career path, lifestyle choice, or relationships, the Ace of Cups advises you to make the choice that best supports your relationships, promotes the values of love, beauty, and harmony, and supports your personal, inner-world values.

The reversed appearance of this card calls for emotional restraint. You can examine and acknowledge emotions that surface, but now is not a good or appropriate time for expressing them too intensely or openly; you must be guarded and reserved. This also suggests a withholding of emotional nutrition. Perhaps you've been giving too much of yourself; you may be wasting love or energy on the wrong person or people, and what you have to offer may not be valued or appreciated. The reversed Ace of Cups may also suggest a need to disassociate from your feelings, perhaps as a requirement for objectivity, or as a temporary coping strategy, if you have feelings or memories that are too painful or overwhelming to confront all at once.

Rider-Waite Tarot

Two of Cups

Golden Dawn Tarot

Love

Sacred CircleTarot

Two of Cups

The Two cards represent the different ways we deal with other people—especially in one-to-one relationships—and sometimes these accommodations present obstacles to the goals and drives signified by the Aces. However, with the Two of Cups, there is a desire for empathy, harmony, and the establishment of emotional bonds, which leads to a very special depth and quality of relationship. Thus, this card signifies friendships, other meaningful partnerships, and even love matches. In Two of Cups situations, rapport with another person makes you feel more complete, more truly yourself. When two people are open to each other's feelings, energy flows between them and they are able to achieve and experience more together than they could separately.

As a card of advice, the Two of Cups affirms all actions and desires to form and maintain meaningful relationships. All decisions must be made on the basis of what will nourish interpersonal bonds and preserve peace and harmony. Of course, balancing the urges of the Self with the demands of the Other requires love and concern, as well as restraint, negotiation, and compromise. The full expression of emotional urges hinted at in the Ace of Cups is somewhat curtailed. Naturally, this card promotes love and marriage, and the cooperation and mutuality that such unions require. It also advises you to connect with new people. For people who are lonely or bored, it suggests seeking out kindred spirits.

Generally, to deal with the matters in question, be cooperative and treat all people involved in a very considerate and personal manner, on a one-to-one basis, if possible. Your gestures and actions should extend good will and promote good feelings. If you are dealing with difficult people, or enemies, you must find a way to turn them into friends and allies, even if you must give something up. Try to achieve a meeting of the minds and focus on shared ideals and purposes. The Two of Cups represents reciprocity in relationships, recognizing that people can create important bonds by doing small favors and, in turn, asking small favors of one another. Cultivate and practice this form of give and take. Your situation may require that you ask for help from someone close to you. If you are the kind of person who is afraid to impose on others—perhaps an introvert—this is a time in life to reach out to your friends and allow yourself to lean on them a little (within reasonable bounds). If you're shy about doing this, commit yourself to ways that you can reciprocate the favors.

You may also apply this card's advice by regenerating your existing relationships, especially your bond with your significant other. In *Gift from the Sea*, Anne Morrow

Lindbergh explains that two people experience a certain purity and simplicity when their relationship is new, stating, "the simplicity of first love, or friendliness, the mutuality of first sympathy seems, at its initial appearance . . . to be a self-enclosed world," or a "magical closed circle." However, that feeling is lost as the partners become encumbered by their functional roles, that is, their work-a-day roles. Lindbergh claims that this is true of the relationship between two buddies or between parent and child, but that this change is especially felt between husband and wife "because it is the deepest one, and the most arduous to maintain." She suggests that couples go off on vacations or outings alone together (without the kids and other distractions) to recapture some of the quality of that original uncomplicated togetherness. She adds that it's also a good idea to give each child some special time alone to reexperience "the pure relationship he once had with the mother, when he was the 'baby'" (pp. 65–71).

When the Two of Cups comes up reversed, consider whether you've been over-committing yourself to too many individuals, and, as a result, making promises you can't fulfill and letting down the people who really are important to you. It may be necessary to redefine your boundaries and renegotiate your relationships with respect to how much you will commit and to whom. Although the reversed Two of Cups suggests maintaining relationships, it may advise withdrawing somewhat from at least a few relationships to increase your personal space and improve your perspective. With respect to some friendships or business partnerships, you may want to stay in the relationship for practical reasons, but don't put your whole heart into it. Also, this is not a good time to reach an agreement, strike a bargain, or form a new partnership. There is an indication that personalities are not well matched.

Three
of
Cups

Rider-Waite Tarot

THREE

Witches Tarot

THREE OF CUPS

THE DRESSING OF THE
SACRED SPRING

Legend Tarot

Three of Cups

The Three of Cups is a card that relates to three big C's: celebration, community, and communication. This card shows how we can communicate good feelings through celebration—and celebration is all the more meaningful when shared with community.

When the Three of Cups comes up in an advice reading, there are a lot of things you can do to spread the good feelings it expresses. You can start by communicating any good news or other joys you have to share. Make calls or write letters to the people you care about, mindful of the old English proverb, "A sorrow that's shared is but half a trouble, But a joy that's shared is a joy made double" (Ray, *The Home Book of Quotations*, p. 1019). Let your words and actions show your joy in others' good fortune when they share their own news with you. Your network of communication is a very special type of community, and the circulation of positive messages builds and fortifies it.

As a card that celebrates our connectedness with others, the Three of Cups especially signifies our relationship to our most immediate communities: those of our family affiliations and those of personal choice. It recommends nurturing your emotional support systems by bringing family and friends together for pleasurable experiences where all can relate from the heart. Naturally, this card also advises accepting invitations and taking advantage of other social opportunities. Think about ways to reach out to more people. Because Threes are cards of creativity and synthesis, they also suggest bringing different types of people together. Introduce friends to other friends, and ask your friends to introduce you to new people, too. Broaden your community of choice for the creative results this will produce.

The Three of Cups suggests participating in celebrational activities and events that engage an even larger community. You might want to attend local festivals and other enjoyable community activities that promote ideals and goals. When larger communities are able to ritualize celebratory occasions, they create bonds and affirm shared values; this generates cooperation and trust, and helps divergent elements within the community come together in harmony and celebration. A modern application of the Three of Cups card is the social interaction and celebrations that take place at the office. The office serves as an important community for many people, filling the role that neighborhoods once did.

Of course, you don't always have to celebrate in the company of other people. You can do little things that please you, things that are playful, pleasurable, and make you feel more alive, as a way of affirming accomplishments and other good things in your life. Also, you don't have to celebrate a specific achievement or event—sometimes you can just celebrate the sheer joy of life! Many of us are not willing to set aside time for the type of pleasurable, celebrational activities denoted by the Three of Cups because we feel overwhelmed by our work and all of the other demands that are put on us. However, recreation and enjoyment of social pleasures generate creative energy that carries over into our work and other aspects of daily life, enabling us to accomplish more, and to bring a better quality to our efforts and products. Stretch the good feelings depicted by the Three of Cups by carrying a celebrational attitude throughout your week. Be imaginative in looking for little things to celebrate, and cultivate the attitude that life itself is a celebration.

The popular illustration for this card, that of three maidens dancing, calls the image of the three Graces to mind. These three Greek goddesses personified abundance, radiance, and joy, and "represent the delight in living that produces art, dance, music, and love" (Monaghan, *The Book of Goddesses and Heroines*, p. 136). These relate to the values and refinements we often describe as culture, so the Three of Cups advocates a graceful lifestyle. Emulate this card by seeking and cultivating the things of high culture.

As a card of general advice, the Three of Cups suggests that you choose in favor of jobs and other options that are socially fulfilling, that allow you to be among your own kind of people, and that enable you to bring grace and beauty into your daily life. Also, you can work a little imitative magic here; if there is something you want to bring into your life, have a party or do something special to celebrate it as if it has already happened!

When the Three of Cups comes up reversed in a reading for advice, it may indicate that although you should continue to nurture your social bonds, there is a possibility that your outside activities are interfering with your work, studies, or other responsibilities, so you need to cut back a bit. You may need to be more selective. Perhaps the people you work or associate with are all very nice people, but they are not nourishing your spirit. If this is the case, you need to seek out kindred spirits, find your own people, and do what you can to create your own community of choice. Here, you want to emphasize quality over quantity in your friendships and social dealings.

Rider-Waite Tarot

four
of
Cups

THE FADING
FELLOWSHIP

Legend Tarot

Celtic Dragon Tarot

four of Cups

Because the Fours represent security and stability, and the Cups represent the emotional and spiritual life, the Four of Cups denotes a period of calm and a safe and peaceful space, whether it be an attitude or a physical place. This is a state of feeling "at home," emotionally settled in, secure, and at peace. Angeles Arrien recognizes this when she says that this card, labeled "Luxury" in the Thoth deck, represents "the experience of feeling emotionally fulfilled and satisfied" (*The Tarot Handbook*, p. 167). However, Pamela Colman Smith, who designed the Waite deck, which is widely used, featured a discontented-looking man in her illustration of the Four of Cups. Consequently, this card is usually interpreted to mean dissatisfaction and boredom. It could be said that there is something in human nature that craves stimulation and change, and that we tend to become discontent when things are too peaceful and stable. At the same time, we can lapse into patterns of habit that prevent us from getting up and doing anything to bring new experiences into life.

As a card of advice, you can interpret the Four of Cups in two different ways depending on whether the image of peace or of dissatisfaction is featured in the deck you use, or seems to resonate more to your question or your situation.

In the first case, this card, broadly applied, advises you to promote peace and stability, being sure to respect your own emotional needs as well as the feelings of the people around you. If you have consulted the Tarot about making a decision, the Four of Cups advises you to choose in favor of options that preserve the status quo and keep your home, family, and relationships in tact. Security issues may be important here, so do what you can to assure that these needs are met.

The second interpretation applies if you have been feeling unsettled and bothered about things you can't pinpoint. Question your motivations and look more deeply within to understand some of the root causes of your beliefs and behavior, as well as to discover your sources of energy and joy. Here, this card tells us that contentment is not the same as complacency, and stirs the kind of discontent that pushes us to self-discovery. If you are in a life situation in which the things that formerly gave you pleasure are no longer able to motivate you, find a new interest or rekindle an old one. Ask yourself whether you have been spending enough time with pursuits that fulfill the needs of your core self. Try meditation as a means of rediscovering what your genuine needs and wants may be. You can emulate the figure in the picture by detaching, disengaging, and getting yourself to a quiet place where you can think.

If you are trying to make a decision or plan a course of action, further investigation or contemplation is advised. Allow some time to pass, and important facts or considerations will surface. However, bear in mind that while passing time in the Four of Cups state, the blues may settle in, causing you to see things in a negative light. It is important to maintain your objectivity. If you have consulted the Tarot for help in choosing from a number of options, the Four of Cups implies that you should choose the one most likely to give you deep-down soul satisfaction, even if other factors argue against it.

If you have consulted the Tarot because you wish to know whether to commit to a relationship, the Four of Cups suggests that you examine your motivations and consider waiting until you know your own mind better. Perhaps the relationship gives you some measure of comfort and security, but fails to satisfy you on a deeper level. The presence of this card indicates that if there is a problem in a relationship, the problem is primarily with you, and it is within yourself that the changes will need to be made.

If you seek the Tarot's advice out of concern for your health, the Four of Cups tells you to open to your intuition (in addition, of course, to seeking whatever professional care is called for) to help discern what course of treatment to pursue. Our bodies have what might be called a *somatic consciousness* that knows what is wrong and where the problem is, and can even sense what substance or action will correct the condition. To open to the body's wisdom, relax (don't strain), and wait for whatever gut feelings, dreams, or flashes of insight present themselves.

When the Four of Cups pertains to an emotionally self-contained, but static, state of being, the reversed card may advise coming out of your shell or other secure space and opening up emotionally to get stimulation and feedback from others. When this card comes up, it may also indicate that you've been overly cautious and hesitant, and now is the time to make a decision or take action, even if you feel unprepared. What decision should you make? Choose the course of action that best satisfies your core creativity. What if this doesn't apply? Then flip a coin or toss the dice—chances are that things will work out better than if you had continued to debate about it.

five
of
Cups

Rider-Waite Tarot

FIVE OF CUPS

LANCELOT & ELAINE

Legend Tarot

Celtic Dragon Tarot

five of Cups

The Five of Cups relates to processes of change that affect the inner life, often disrupting emotionally comfortable situations. Discontent and a desire for meaning (as incipient, but below the surface, in the previous card, the Four of Cups), may compel people to look for fulfillment outside of the boundaries of their normal lives, relationships, and routines. However, it is difficult to make changes without doing damage, to experiment without incurring regrets and losses, to move in new directions without a loss of security. Consequently, many versions of this card depict a man standing in an attitude of grief or regret, with three overturned cups at his feet (while two upright cups stand unnoticed behind him). Change is emotionally disorienting, so there are apt to be emotional highs and lows, mood swings, and shifting emotions and instability, especially since the sense of uncertainty denoted by the Five of Cups may stir up feelings, causing a person to relive old issues and dwell on new regrets.

The cards in the Cups suit correspond to our emotional lives and the quality of our relationships. The Five of Cups deals with the element of change in relationships. Some interpreters see the disconsolate figure in the card illustration as a person grieving for the loss of love; certainly, the Fives' impetus to change is going to impose stress on a relationship. Sometimes, when we make choices for change in our inner or outer lives (or both, inasmuch as inner and outer conditions mirror each other and interrelate), we come to the realization that our relationships must also change, or at least accommodate our growth, or else be left behind. This is particularly true when there is something fundamentally wrong in the relationship, such as abusive, codependent, or other dysfunctional situations. Applied as a card of advice, the Five of Cups may call for you to make tough choices in favor of actions and conditions that nurture your soul but may require severing or distancing yourself from certain relationships. It is important here to use wisdom and uphold your values so you don't injure your loved ones and discard meaningful and worthwhile relationships in the pursuit of sensation and novelty.

Otherwise, applied as a card of general advice, the Five of Cups calls for stimulation, challenge, and change—especially in the inner life. Decide in favor of career options, lifestyles, and other major life choices that will take you in new directions, expose you to new sensations and experiences, and test your character and beliefs, even if this means going through a stressful or unsettled phase. You can focus on the positive qualities of the Five of Cups symbolism by finding ways to bring new things into your emotional and spiritual life—things that stimulate creativity and growth.

It is probably best to seek social stimulation and new friendships outside of your family and your normal circles of acquaintance, though you can find ways to involve your loved ones in these positive changes so the exploration of new feelings can be a shared experience. Again, if you want to look for love, go outside the boundaries of your normal associations, especially by becoming involved in stimulating activities where you can meet interesting people. To hold on to love or improve existing relationships, be creative in bringing excitement into your relationships.

As you work to bring change to your home situation, work life, and so on, be aware that in trying new things and engaging in creative experimentation, there is typically some waste of time, energy, and money. We have to allay these regrets by accepting that a certain amount of waste is part of the creative process. Accept that mistakes, embarrassment, and losses are part of a natural process, part of the flow of life, without which we cannot go forward.

When the Five of Cups card is reversed, the Tarot may be telling you that it is necessary to seek change, but at a slower, more gentle pace in order to honor your commitments and protect your existing relationships.

Rider-Waite Tarot

Six of Cups

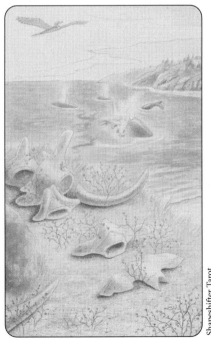

Shapeshifter Tarot

Golden Dawn Tarot

Six of Cups

The Six of Cups represents a peaceful interlude: a time and place where creative energy can flow and the mind can turn to aesthetic pleasures and other pursuits that enhance the quality of our inner as well as outer environments.

As a card of advice, the Six of Cups encourages you to set emotional riches and quality of life as your main priorities. Participate in pleasurable social activities and make choices in favor of jobs and other life options that allow you a higher degree of leisure and pleasure. Naturally, this card is in favor of decisions to take a vacation or an early retirement. It also encourages creative and artistic activities and lifestyles. The Six of Cups is concerned with the quality of one's surroundings, so you might do what you can to bring beauty and harmony into your personal space, and, in line with Cups values, find ways to share this space with loved ones (especially young people). Incidentally, this card is sometimes related to our idealized notions of country living, and may have a special message if you are thinking about moving to a rural or resort area.

The peaceful state that the Six of Cups evokes suggests some of our romanticized memories and ideals of childhood, which may be why the Waite deck's illustration features two children gathering flowers in what appears to be a castle garden. Many interpretations focus on children, children's concerns, the joys of childhood, and childhood memories. Therefore, this card's advice applies to questions revolving around children, and favors decisions to have children, work with children, reunite with childhood friends, return to the scenes of childhood, or reacquaint yourself with your childhood hobbies or ambitions. You might also want to reexperience some of the little pleasures you had as a child, or perhaps do or buy something special to make up for something you feel you missed out on as a child. If you have children of your own, do what you can to create some very positive experiences for them, and don't put off opportunities for shared activities.

If you know what sort of activities gave you joy as a child, this is a key to recapturing lost fragments of your Self, so try to revive some of your old interests. The garden pictured in this card is a sort of enclosure. You can build for yourself a metaphorical enclosure in which to reexplore and recapture some of the feelings, beliefs, talents, and other simple joys you knew as a child. Do this by seeking out people and places where you feel safe to be yourself, to express the spontaneous, but vulnerable, natural child in you.

The number six has artistic affinities, so the Six of Cups also recommends time set aside for creative pleasures. In keeping with the conventional meaning of this card, you might want to look to your childhood (or an ideal of childhood) for inspiration. As Rainer Maria Rilke advised a young poet, "even if you were in some prison the walls of which let none of the sounds of the world come to your senses—would you not then still have your childhood, that precious, kingly possession, that treasure-house of memories? Turn your attention thither" (*Letters to a Young Poet*, p. 18).

The Six of Cups' concern with the things of childhood and of the past have some negative implications. Some people can't find happiness because they cling to an ideal of how things ought to be, related to their images of a golden childhood (real or imagined), which they are trying to recapture. Likewise, some people wallow in memories and emotions of childhood victimization, using them as justification for selfishness, self-indulgence, inaction, and irresponsibility. Unfortunately, when our hearts or minds are in the past, our energy is also in the past. This loss of vitality prevents us from living in our bodies and grasping the pleasures of the moment. (No wonder the Victorians classified nostalgia as a disease.) In an advice reading, the reversed Six of Cups could therefore counsel us to put away some (not all) of the things of childhood, and to get down to the business of creating a beautiful life in the present. You can find ways to bring sentimental pleasures into your work life and home life, but break with any indulgences that rob you of the present.

Seven
of
Cups

Rider–Waite Tarot

Celtic Dragon Tarot

Legend Tarot

Seven of Cups

The Seven of Cups relates to the life of the imagination, and portrays an inner world enriched by dreams, fantasies, and spiritual meanings. Its usual illustration shows visions of wonder that pour forth from seven cups that are suspended in the air. This card expresses itself in simple fantasies, as well as in mystical and spiritual experiences.

Writers on the Tarot often view the Seven of Cups somewhat negatively, as denoting time wasted on daydreams and illusions. In an ordinary Tarot reading, the Seven of Cups would bode ill for involvement in projects, investments, love relationships, etc., warning of possible delusions. However, in the context of an advice reading, this card recommends bringing a touch of fantasy and the element of the unexpected into your relationships and other activities in order to revitalize your sense of possibility and to help you work toward making dreams come true. This card especially promotes creative work, urging you to find creative outlets where you can let your imagination flow.

The Seven of Cups also suggests changing your way of seeing things. Put on some rose-colored glasses or try to see things from a new perspective, perhaps from a child's point of view.

If you have concerns about a failing business, project, or relationship, the problem may be with your vision for it, that is, the lack of a motivating and unifying vision. This card suggests a need to have a dream, a guiding image as a star to which you can hitch your wagon. In relationships, it's important that there be a shared vision. On the other hand, if lack of vision is not the problem, perhaps you are divided between too many aspirations, and a sorting-out process will be needed—you'll have to decide which of your dreams will be the most meaningful to follow. You'll also need some resolve to bring your dreams into reality. Look to the Seven of Pentacles for perseverance and the Seven of Wands for conviction.

The escapist delights conjured by the Seven of Cups may be suggested as a remedy for problems related to stress, fatigue, and other sorts of physical and psychological problems. This card is likely to appear in advice readings for people who have been too weighed down by responsibilities, or too distracted by the cares of the world. If you feel that you don't have a right to indulge in a little escapism, this card gives you permission.

On a deeper level, the Seven of Cups speaks to the needs of the mind, spirit, and soul, all of which are nourished by the imagination and the experience of wonder. If you have been feeling stressed or depressed, or are suffering from a loss of direction and meaning, this card suggests refocusing on your inner life. Signe Echols and her coauthors of *Spiritual Tarot* point out that the fantastical objects emanating from the floating cups can represent "elements of your being," including contents of your shadow "that need to be acknowledged, examined, and dealt with or honored" (pp. 186–87). You might want to get into meditation, dream analysis, psychotherapy, and/or spiritual disciplines that help you explore your inner world. Seek out the sort of experiences that make you feel mystically and spiritually attuned. No matter how skeptical or disillusioned you may be, engage in magical thinking, that willing suspension of disbelief, as a way of connecting with the spiritual world, and act *as if* miracles and fantastical things are real.

When the Seven of Cups presents itself reversed, it may suggest that you need to make more realistic plans. You may have to downsize your vision, at least for the time being. Note that it does not mean that you have to give up your dreams, just bring them more in line with what is doable for you now. Rather than changing your life to pursue a fantasy, you may have to rework the fantasy in a way that brings meaning into your ordinary life.

There are some people who are so focused on intellectual, mystical, or spiritual things that they neglect or devalue their physical needs as well as the affairs of the work-a-day world. If this is a problem for you, the reversed Seven of Cups suggests that you express your inner-world values in outer-world interactions. Find ways to bring a little magic into mundane routines so that you get more accomplished, but accomplished with style. If you can remember interesting images and objects from your dreams or fantasies, find some way to reproduce and display them in your waking life. Be sure to maintain meaningful dialogues and relationships with other people, too, as a means of grounding and reality testing.

Rider-Waite Tarot

Eight
of
Cups

Witches Tarot

EIGHT

Legend Tarot

Eight of Cups

The Eight of Cups represents the organization of the inner life, and pertains to relationships and emotional response patterns that have become fixed in place. This may denote an emotional existence that is comfortable, peaceful, orderly, and whole unto itself—often the product of self-control and the ability to learn from experience. However, the state of order that is imposed on the feelings may also stifle vitality and intensity of personal expression, leading to boredom and inertia. The pictorial image often associated with this card, that of a man turning his back on a group of cups and wandering off into the distance, may portray an underlying desire to regenerate the life of the spirit by seeking change.

When the Eight of Cups comes up in an advice reading, you might first assess the state of your emotional affairs and their correspondence with the other aspects of your life, including your soul life, in keeping with this card's basic concern with order. The best way to do this is to mentally detach and step outside yourself to review your accumulation of memories and feelings. (This is a process that many of us go through, often in middle age, when we try to make sense of it all, to look for the deeper meanings in our experiences, and to decide where to go from here.) If you find that things are in a state of chaos, and that you haven't done the best job of learning from experiences, it is probably best to act out the numerological meaning of this card by working at creating stable inner and outer environments. Make decisions and choices that preserve order and balance, even if doing so requires suppression of some impulses and desires. Along with this, do what you can to nurture emotional relationships as a way of weaving the net of mutual obligations that help to structure a productive life. On the other hand, if you have fallen into the doldrums and feel oppressed by the demands of your emotional networks, think about ways to bring emotional stimulation and spiritual nourishment into your life.

Depending on the nature of your question and your circumstances, some advice interpretations may refer directly to this card's graphic representation. For example, if you have asked a specific question about whether you should travel, move to another location, or leave a particular situation, the Eight of Cups probably advises in favor of this, related to its common graphic portrayal of a man with a walking stick who has crossed a river and is wandering off into the distance.

When you draw the reversed Eight of Cups, the Tarot may suggest that this is a time to analyze the ways that your feeling reflexes have locked you into certain behavior patterns and complexes, and to think about ways to break patterns that are undesirable, or to replace compulsions with more consciously approved behaviors.

The reversed Eight of Cups may also come up at times when life seems to be too settled, too flat, when you're consciously or unconsciously longing for some stimulation or change. Sometimes this leads to a decision (or at least a desire) to leave a relationship. Sometimes a person becomes ensconced in a matrix of binding relationships and may dream of escape, though he or she is also subject to a certain inertia that discourages real attempts at change. If the problem is just boredom with a life that is too programmed and ordered, a temporary getaway may be a solution. In the end, you can return to your established equilibrium, and also bring something back with you—interesting new experiences that enrich the whole. You can also enliven your situation by bringing the imaginative experiences of the Seven of Cups into your relationships, or by focusing on the varied pleasures hinted at in the Nine of Cups. You should consider the possibility of abandoning your situation only if you are in an abusive relationship or work environment, or any other situation where your personal needs are discounted.* However, if your life and your relationships are generally wholesome and worth preserving, give further consideration to the security and tranquility potential of this card. Weigh and evaluate your desire for stimulation against the need to maintain order and stability in your life.

* Because the Eights can sometimes represent organized systems that are somewhat inflexible, they can denote dysfunctional systems. In the Eight of Cups, this can relate to dysfunctional families. Therapist-author John Bradshaw characterizes the dysfunctional family as a system that is closed in on itself, rigid in its rules, and unable to tolerate difference or negotiate conflict. The patriarch or matriarch usually sets the rules, which assert "It's my way or the highway" (*On: The Family*, audiotape). Seen from this angle, the figure in the Eight of Cups could represent the individual who decides to leave a stifling emotional situation and take to the highway.

Nine
of
Cups

Rider-Waite Tarot

Witches Tarot

NINE

Shapeshifter Tarot

Nine of Cups

The Nine of Cups represents the multiplication of emotional riches that result in a special quality of life. Although common illustrations of this card, which show a fat man enjoying his abundance, tend to emphasize physical pleasures, this card also speaks to the life of the spirit. It denotes a state in which one's inner and outer worlds are working together, dynamically and creatively, to manifest happiness, abundance, and the fulfillment of desires.

When the Nine of Cups comes up in a reading, it often pertains to issues of entitlement to happiness versus issues of deprivation and lack of deserving. Some people feel that they don't deserve happiness due to guilt or low self-esteem, or they may have been inculcated with different forms of cultural puritanism and beliefs in "limited good." When people have a belief in limited good, they fear that if they enjoy themselves too much, something bad will happen later on, or there will be deprivation in some other area. If such beliefs are holding you back, the Nine of Cups urges you to enjoy life and go after whatever you believe will bring you happiness (providing that it doesn't involve hurting anyone, since you can't build genuine happiness on another person's misery). Express joy and pleasure freely in the knowledge that this will increase your happiness, which will enable you to manifest even greater good.

In some illustrations of the Nine of Cups, the human figure sits before shelves lined with cups, suggesting that he may be an innkeeper or generous host. This also depicts the multiplication of happiness because joys increase when they are shared. Therefore, this card advises in favor of decisions and other actions that enable you to extend hospitality to others. On a larger scale, it recommends adopting the attitude of cosmic hospitality, opening your heart to the living universe.

In keeping with the interest in lifestyles and the portrayal of solitary figures in the Nine cards, the Nine of Cups also encourages your enjoyment of personal pleasures, even when there is no one with whom to share them. Some of us feel that we can't justify indulging in certain pleasures unless there is a special occasion and others are there to partake. This card tells us that we can enjoy luxuries even if no one else is around. Sometimes it's necessary for us to give ourselves permission to indulge a little in order to avoid sinking into a deprivation mentality.

The physicality depicted in many popular illustrations of this card may also have philosophical significance and offer advice for living well. Puritanical attitudes have influenced our relationships to our own bodies, and have shaped society's prejudice against people deemed to be overweight. While overindulgence is certainly harmful to the individual, the mortification of the flesh that has been driven by fashion consciousness and other pressures to maintain a certain look has also brought about great misery and undermined many peoples' ability to achieve the sort of robust health that is necessary for maintaining the harmony of body and spirit. Since the Nine of Cups teaches that pleasure generates enthusiasm for life, it encourages you to take pleasure in your own body and the things of the body, and not to disdain your physical nature.

In teaching that physical enjoyment is necessary to personal vitality, this card also advocates that you engage in the activities that you know will rekindle your enthusiasm, even if you are reluctant to do so until all of your work is done. Unfortunately, since work is never done, you may never have any fun. When this happens, you can become weary and manifest a host of minor aches and illnesses, with the result that even less gets done. Your Tarot mentor wants you to know that by setting time aside for things that are enjoyable and personally fulfilling, you will have more energy, enabling you to get more accomplished and to turn in a higher quality of work.

When the Nine of Cups comes up reversed in an advice reading, it may suggest that while you should continue to enjoy the good things of life, it would be a good idea to practice more self-restraint, to work for more delayed rewards. It is possible that some of your actions have been driven by a needy inner child; although it is necessary to reassure the inner child and allow it some indulgences, there also comes a time when more mature facets of the personality be allowed to take over and guide you into the future.

Rider-Waite Tarot

Ten
of
Cups

Sacred Circle Tarot

Celtic Dragon Tarot

Ten of Cups

The Ten of Cups applies to emotional matters within one's circle of relationships. The traditional associations apply especially to families, but this card may also refer to community-oriented ideals, involving other groups where members form strong bonds with each other. It betokens an abundance of love and good feelings, made possible in a group where individuals' personal qualities, interests, and feelings are respected and valued. When loving ideals are part of a group's values and traditions, these good feelings can bridge many generations and extend outward to influence the general well-being of a society.

Generally, this card advises you to promote the unity and well-being of your family or family-like group. Make decisions and choices that favor the making and preservation of relationships, and the expansion of both family and social circles. Work toward achieving your idealized image of family, and be lavish in extending expressions of love, appreciation, and encouragement to everyone. Spend quality time with your family or group engaged in "heart" activities—activities where good feelings are freely and openly generated and shared. Since it can be said that a family is a group of people who share certain rituals, plan activities that maintain the family or group as a community of celebration. In addition to such get-togethers, carry out kin-keeping chores that keep everyone in touch, such as sending out holiday cards and congratulations, attending young peoples' recitals, and other activities that celebrate and affirm members' interests and accomplishments. The Ten of Cups can also stand for the expansion of one's circle to allow new cycles of interaction, so think about ways you can stretch your emotional boundaries to include new people with new outlooks and enthusiasm.

If you have approached the Tarot for advice on dealing with personal worries or sorrows, this card advises you to call upon your family (or group) network for emotional support. The emotional fulfillment promised by the Ten of Cups may also be achieved by seeking or creating a "family of choice," a term used by John Bradshaw (*Homecoming*, p. 209). Today, many people have come to realize that their biological families are often unwilling or unable to support them in their needs for personal expression and growth, and so they're turning to support groups of all sorts, including religious groups, cyberfamilies, and other larger circles of friends and kindred spirits for nurturing fellowship. Despite some of its other drawbacks, our modern society does facilitate the creation of new families and communities by providing extensive systems of communication.

Where difficult decisions and choices are concerned, you would be urged to put family and group needs ahead of personal ones, with special attention to the emotional needs of others and the long-term consequences. However, if an intergenerational conflict is involved, choices have to be made that best support the growth needs of the young, even if at the expense of boyfriends, girlfriends, spouses, parents, or even grandparents, in keeping with the Tens concern for new cycles and new generations. As an old Chinese proverb says, "Tears fall downward." In other words, there are some circumstances where you have to put your children ahead of your partners, parents, or others. If you have consulted the Tarot about a dispute over inheritance or the division of property, this card counsels you to put collective interests ahead of your personal ones. The preservation of the family's emotional support network is more valuable than individual gains.

When the Ten of Cups is reversed, it suggests that while you should continue to honor your relationships, there may be a need for emotional distancing from family or friends. Perhaps you have become emotionally overdependent on others, or it may be that you need to stay objective in order to avoid being caught up in family disputes or bogged down in their emotional morasses. Consider ways in which you can promote the collective well-being while maintaining your own boundaries.

In some cases, the questioner's problems may stem from clinging to an ideal of the happy family. It may be necessary to give the image of the perfect parents and family back to the mythological world. Come to an acceptance that your family may not be the family you wanted, and then focus on the good things that it does have to offer. This does not suggest that you reject your family of origin, but rather, learn to feel okay about it.

Page
of
Cups

Page of Cups

Pages represent the need to open to new experiences, and in an advice reading, the Page of Cups encourages you to explore the realm of the emotions and the spirit, especially by opening yourself to your own feelings and to the feelings of others. This means making yourself more vulnerable—do not be afraid to take this risk.

It is the Page's sympathetic imagination, his ability to put himself into another person's place, so to speak, that creates empathy, care, and understanding. This card recommends putting yourself in learning situations where you can become more attuned to the needs of others. You might try volunteer work as a way of learning to work with and relate to people, as well as a means of making a place for yourself in your community. This card may also advise that you find a friend and fellow learner who shares your inner-world values. You can gain greater personal insight by relating your spiritual and emotional discoveries to a sympathetic friend.

The Page of Cups is immersed in an inner world of emotions, ideals, and imaginings, and this is a necessary part of his identity growth. This card may, therefore, advise you to engage in dream work, active imagination, and other means of gaining personal knowledge.

The Pages have a special function as cards of communication, so the Page of Cups suggests that you deal with a situation in question by communicating your feelings. This especially indicates warm feelings such as love, care, compassion, and appreciation, as well as the gestures and other body language that go with these emotions. However, you should also express your personal needs and speak up about anything that is disturbing or hurting you. For "thinking people," and others who are not as adept at expressing themselves as "feeling people," this may be awkward and embarrassing, and may seem like learning a whole new language (especially for those who tend to scoff at touchy-feely stuff). For help in adapting to this mode of communication, listen to the words of people you know, as well as public personalities, who are very effective in creating trust, empathy, and good feelings through their style of relating and speaking. Also, explore the ways in which you can use different means of communication, such as intimate conversations, letter writing, and phone calls to create closer bonds with the people you care about.

Open expression and depth of feeling are a part of the Page of Cups' natural charm. However, there are times in life when we have to manage our moods and suppress some feelings. If you draw the Page of Cups reversed in an advice reading, the Tarot may be suggesting that the situation in question requires you to exercise mood control, perhaps to get something done or to deal with the emotional needs of others. Use the Page of Cups' capacity for empathy to understand why the focus has to be on the feelings of others, at least for the time being.

Another problem with Page of Cups types is that their normal sensitivity, openness, naiveté, and desire to please make them vulnerable to criticism, rejection, and forms of exploitation. Such people adapt to meet the expectations of others—often acting on unspoken signals—so there is a danger of identity loss. When this card comes up reversed, it may suggest that you hold on to the Page's interpersonal values, but be more detached and objective so you don't care as much about what other people think and don't take things personally.

Rider-Waite Tarot

Knight
of
Cups

Legend Tarot

GALAHAD

Celtic Dragon Tarot

Knight of Cups

The Knight of Cups heralds active and passionate engagement (especially with other people) in the realm of feelings. This Knight is motivated by eros, which is the desire to seek wholeness through union with another. This impulse can be expressed through erotic love, but it also promotes feelings of unity on a broader scale, creating a sense of relationship with all our fellow humans and with the world of nature. The Knight of Cups embodies that aspect of the Self that Moore and Gillette, in their study of masculine archetypes, call "the lover." When this card comes up in an advice reading, consider the ways in which you can embody the spirit and power of love, care, and empathy. Immerse yourself in that mode of feeling, and then take it out into the world. The Knight of Cups can be a spiritual warrior, or simply a person who cares and is willing to get involved.

The Knight of Cups pursues and acts on emotional desires, so this card is often said to predict a love affair. If you have approached the Tarot with questions about getting involved in a relationship, this card is definitely in favor of it. The Knight of Cups urges wholehearted involvement in loving relationships of all sorts, and tells you that it's okay to be open, affectionate, sentimental, and passionate. Don't be afraid to take risks in love or to wear your heart on your sleeve, if you want to. If there seem to be no prospects for love in your current situation or environment, go out and look for them.

You can also interpret the Knight of Cups as encouraging all other pursuits for which you have a passion—the things that make you feel playful, young, and alive. Knights can show movement toward or away from different people or things, so when this card is part of a layout, pay attention to any other cards toward which the Knight of Cups is facing. This may tell you something about the nature of any relationship or activity the Tarot advises pursuing.

Another way to take up the Knight of Cups theme is to involve others in feeling experiences by inviting or accompanying friends to pleasant social gatherings and outings. Do things that are mutually enjoyable and just for fun, that make you feel like a bunch of kids again. In line with Cups values, you might also plan activities that create or enhance a sense of community. Also, seek the companionship of people who are fun to be with and perhaps already active in social and community-building efforts.

Knights represent involvement, while reversed cards suggest holding something back, so the reversed Knight of Cups may advise restraining the intensity of your involvement in emotional and spiritual affairs. This could mean that you should have only a platonic relationship with someone you are attracted to. It might also mean that you should not allow yourself to be swept away by emotions or religious devotion, and limit the amount of energy you put into causes, for fear of losing your integrity and identity.

The same sensitivity and romanticism that can make Cups personalities so charming can also make them ineffective in managing real-world concerns. If this card comes up reversed in a reading, you have possibly lapsed into negative Cups behaviors such as escapism and addiction. Hold on to your romantic ideals, but find ways to integrate the energetic, action-oriented behavior of the Knight of Wands and the tough-minded views of the Knight of Swords into your strategy for dealing with life's challenges.

Queen
of
Cups

Queen of Cups

When the Queen of Cups comes up in an advice reading, you are urged to exercise your personal power, charm, and understanding in your relationships with people—especially those closest to you. Develop the Queen of Cups' unique ability to make other people feel special; give them the full focus of your attention, sympathy, understanding, admiration, and appreciation. This Queen takes a genuinely personal interest in those around her, and her priority is on maintaining peace and harmony in relationships—which is what the Tarot here suggests as the best way to deal with problems and problem people.

To emulate the Queen of Cups' personality traits, be generous with your time, encouragement, and companionship. She nurtures a special vision for those she loves, and will support them in pursuing their dreams, whatever those dreams may be.

The Queen of Cups is also concerned with creating a beautiful home life, so think about making your environment a place that provides spiritual and emotional comfort. Bring in nourishing food, entertainment, and beautiful things for their uplifting effect.

This card also advises cultivating your inner life. The Queen of Cups achieves personal empowerment through dream analysis, meditation, spiritual discipline, and other forms of inner work. Use your Queen of Cups intuition to make decisions based on inner values and directives rather than on what is fashionable, or what our larger society deems to be "for your own good."

All of the Queens relate to functions of mothering, but when we think of the sentimental ideal of "the good mother," we are most likely to picture a Queen of Cups type of personality: she has an indulgent and self-sacrificing nature, and she loves unconditionally. If you have approached the Tarot with questions about relationships, the Queen of Cups urges you to model this ideal in your relationships with others. The appearance of the Queen of Cups may also suggest that you seek comfort and inspiration from a person who supports and understands your emotional needs.

The Queen of Cups is associated with our deep feeling nature, but in our desire to preserve harmony, to be polite, to keep other people cheered, we can lose touch with our own feelings. Thus, a reversed Queen of Cups may be telling you to get reacquainted with your feelings, to truly feel your own feelings. You don't have to give up your concern for other peoples' feelings to do this, just become more observant of your own. Also, Queen of Cups types tend to idealize people, so they are often disappointed or taken advantage of. At the same time, these types may rely too much on other people for personal fulfillment. This can manifest as an extreme neediness that acts like a black hole for sucking in affection and attention. This insatiable need can drive loved ones away. Thus, when this card comes up reversed in an advice reading, it may suggest that you reevaluate the nature of any dependency relationships. Perhaps you need to assess the balance of giving and taking in order to achieve a more wholesome synergy.

Rider-Waite Tarot

King of Cups

Legend Tarot

Golden Dawn Tarot

Minor Arcana: Cups 213

King of Cups

When you draw the King of Cups in an advice reading, the Tarot suggests that you assume a role of benevolent and compassionate leadership in order to deal with the matter at hand. Take charge of situations involving personal relationships, family matters, and community relations. This may also be a time to lend support and guidance to loved ones who are dealing with different spiritual and emotional issues. Don't wait to be asked—use your intuition to sense where your help may be needed. On a broader level, promote the care and well-being of humankind and of the environment. Emulate the King of Cups' leadership style; he is easy-going and democratic, and gives time and attention to the needs and concerns of those who work with him or below him. He is a natural in positions of responsibility when there is a need for someone who can motivate people, bring them together, and reconcile differences.

If you can picture a person, real or imaginary, who exemplifies the quintessential good boss or good father, you are thinking of a King of Cups personality. He is generous in giving encouragement, and people give him loyalty and friendship in return. His ability to acknowledge the accomplishments of others, to extend appreciation and rewards, and to stand back and give others a chance to shine is a mark of true personal empowerment. The appearance of the King of Cups suggests that you emulate these qualities, and perhaps seek help from a mentor who embodies the King of Cups' patience and concern.

The King of Cups card signifies marital and parental love and responsibility, so concern for your loved ones should be a priority and guide any decisions you make. This card counsels in favor of marriage, parenthood, and other family arrangements and duties. This King is concerned with the quality of domestic life, so this card advises you to refocus on matters at home. You can model some of the King of Cups' positive qualities simply by being there for your loved ones. Lend a sympathetic ear with the knowledge that it's not always necessary to fix things; it is your time, understanding, and company that is most valued. This card may also denote a need to put some energy into the sort of household projects that will create a more secure and comfortable home environment.

Since the Cups suit has a special affinity for creative and aesthetic pursuits—especially those that stimulate a sense of unity with the wider world—the King of Cups card urges you to take on some sort of responsibility in an artistic enterprise. Express your personal empowerment through artistic activities and lifestyles, and encourage and promote the same in others.

If you draw the reversed King of Cups in an advice reading, there's an indication that you enjoy popularity and influence with friends and family, but need to divert some of your energies from your home and your social circle in order to assert yourself as a real power in the work world.

A problem with the King of Cups type of person is that he can be an ineffectual leader when, out of a desire to be popular and to avoid confrontations, he is reluctant to take a stand or enforce discipline. Thus, the reversed King of Cups may counsel you to take a tougher stance on the matter in question. You can retain your concern, your civility, and your liking of people while adopting the more competitive techniques of the King of Wands, or the no-nonsense attitude of the King of Swords.

Minor Arcana
Swords

Ace
of
Swords

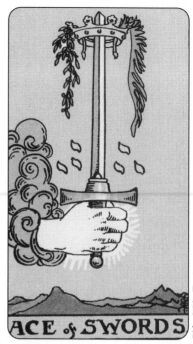

Rider-Waite Tarot

Golden Dawn Tarot

Sacred Circle Tarot

Ace of Swords

Ace cards advise you to express a certain quality of energy through your thoughts and actions. When the Ace of Swords comes up, you will need to bring courage and will power into the realm of action and ideas. You are urged to use a sharp, focused, aggressive energy. You have an opportunity to exercise your personal power and effectiveness in prodding yourself to action, taking on challenges, and solving problems.

The Ace of Swords invokes the clarity of mind and mental focus that penetrates to the heart of a matter. It urges you to map out a strategy in the knowledge that a lot of what you deal with is attitudinal. Don't allow emotions to cloud the reasoning required to cut through problems; apply the full force of your intellect to the situation at hand. The mental energy associated with this card may be linked to the qualities of the archetypal warrior as described by Moore and Gillette. They point out that the warrior uses aggressiveness appropriately when he keeps mind and body focused and alert "through clarity of thinking, through discernment" (*King/Warrior/Magician/Lover*, p. 80). Think back on the times when you were able to think logically while asserting your own position and interests in dealing with conflict. Reexperience this mode of thinking and acting, or emulate people you know who model this savvy, calm, and clear-sightedness.

When Ace of Swords energy is felt, restraints on thought and belief are intolerable. This can manifest itself in the lives of individuals through attempts to break free of dysfunctional home or work situations. As a card of advice, it suggests that you take action, even if it means facing some unpleasantness, to break free of any situations or relationships in which you're not allowed to think for yourself. Because this card teaches that you can take charge of your own thoughts, it also invites you to choose your own reality. Because reality is mutable and malleable, you can decide which terms of reality you wish to operate under. The Ace of Swords' emphasis on free thought and choosing your own operating reality enables you to give yourself an attitude adjustment.

The Ace of Swords brings a force for change that prods us to move forward. Such a motivating force can be uncomfortable, but necessary to arouse and energize us. In the context of an advice reading, you may need to find some way to prod yourself or someone else to action, to get up and get going on the matter in question. This may require some scares or threats if that's what it takes to get the adrenaline going. This card does have a certain urgency to it; there is a need to act in a swift and timely manner. Make haste, take action, act boldly and decisively.

The Ace of Swords' energy is especially needed for problem solving and staving off potential problems. You may have to take the initiative and deal with a problem head on in order to bring an end to it or prevent it from getting worse. Be prepared to encounter trouble, but see that as part of the process. Don't allow setbacks to discourage you. Honor your challenges as teachers.

This card may suggest that you enter a conflict, a battle that you choose to join, perhaps for a worthwhile cause. A show of force or some aggressive action may be necessary to show that you mean business, that you are willing and able to carry out a threat. This may be needed for your own defense in cases where the best defense is a strong offense. This card may also signal the invasion of space—yours or somebody else's. Most aggressive action involves some form of space invasion. Therefore, you are urged to summon the powers of this card when you recognize the need to claim (or reclaim) space that is rightfully your own.

Because the Swords suit emphasizes mental activity, the Ace's advice also suggests that you provide yourself with mental nutrition: seek out the kinds of people, places, activities, or things that keep your mind stimulated.

When the Ace of Swords comes up reversed in an advice reading, there is still a need for aggressive mental energy, but some restraint is called for. Be alert and look for the sources of problems, but avoid direct confrontations. Hold your show of force back, and bide your time.

Rider-Waite Tarot

Two of Swords

Witches Tarot

Celtic Dragon Tarot

Two of Swords

The Two of Swords is a card about negotiating conflict. The appearance of this card will test the quality of your relationships. In a functional family, work team, or in any other healthy system, individual members have the ability to accept and work out differences. If we interpret the central figure in a card as being the questioner engaged in the action that he or she should take, the Two of Swords indicates that you should intervene in the matter in question in an effort to promote equity, mutuality, and understanding.

The Two of Swords challenges your way of thinking because you are confronted with the fact that other people don't see things the same way you do. You are obliged to respect differences in the knowledge that good, honorable people can disagree on major issues. The Two of Swords urges you to become comfortable with differentness or otherness, and learn to live peaceably with people whose natures, lives, beliefs, and experiences are, and always will be, fundamentally different from your own. It's also important to bear in mind that when Sword cards come up, there is an indication that someone has a need to be the winner. The Two of Swords asks you to decide: do you want to be the winner or do you want peace and harmony? It may be better to make some accommodation of other peoples' needs and viewpoints rather than win a victory that just makes a lot of enemies out of the resentful losers.

In an advice reading, this card can apply to contested issues where you are one of the opposing parties, or where you are expected to mediate between different interest groups or factions. In either case, it is up to you to work for a truce. Negotiation and conflict management skills are needed here.

Communication and clarity are important to achieving a working relationship because there has to be a meeting of the minds. The Two of Swords signals a need for the people involved to listen to each other's issues and concerns, make compromises, and find healthy ways to settle their conflicts. For your part, make sure that you have expressed your position clearly, then listen to make sure that you have clearly understood all other positions. Call on the Swords' power of detachment to make sure that you really hear what the other person is saying, which may not be what you are expecting him or her to say. Too often, through prejudice or a need to project our shadow traits, we set other people up as our imagined opponents and impute words and motivations that do not actually belong to them. When we finally get down to hearing and understanding, we may find the basis for disagreement is minor or nonexistent—like arguing apples and oranges.

If you seek to heal conflict, accommodations may need to be made to achieve a working peace. Since the Twos often signify modifying your initial aims, this card suggests trying to meet someone half way on the matter in question. Turn this into a positive by looking for common ground where the parties can work together and promote mutual interests.

If you are in a contested situation where you find it too difficult to be objective, this card could possibly suggest bringing in an arbiter, someone whose good judgment and fair-mindedness you respect. In that case, be willing to bide by his or her suggestions, even if they are not entirely to your liking or advantage.

Generally, the Two of Swords suggests a need to hold off, refrain from making decisions, commitments, involvements, or taking other actions until you can assess others' positions or deal with conflicting factors that may arise to stall your plans and efforts. There are differences that must be dealt with, and, one hopes, worked out. Whether it's upright or in the reversed position, this card bodes ill and advises against getting into more intimate relationships because it denotes a fundamental incompatibility. Even if you work out compromises, things will be uneasy and there will be mutual dissatisfaction.

In addition to dealing with conflict, the Two of Swords offers advice on coming to terms with the dualities, opposition, and contradictions inherent in the human condition. Life puts us into a lot of Catch-22 situations, and we just have to learn to live with that. The figure commonly pictured in this card represents a person who is living with these contradictions—maybe not easily or happily. She is certainly in a tense position, but at the same time, she is not under any threat. The fact that she holds the swords illustrates that she also holds responsibility and power. Her blindfold suggests a coping strategy, perhaps looking inward, taking a philosophical, perhaps even humorous, attitude toward her predicament.

In the reversed position, this card indicates that you have been overcompromised—perhaps you have been giving too much away in your desire to preserve peace and harmony—and now you are advised to break away and assert more of your own rights. You also should withdraw from relationships where there's not enough mutual interest and understanding to arrive at an agreement. Attempts at compromise here may result in a lose-lose situation.

There is another situation in which the reversed Two of Swords' advice applies; sometimes friends, family members, coworkers, or neighbors get into disputes with each other and try to force us to take sides. The Two of Swords is against taking sides, and in the reversed position, it suggests backing out of any involvement at all. Don't feel pressured or guilty; be assured that there is a fundamental wrongness on the part of the other people who try to put you into this position in the first place.

Three
of
Swords

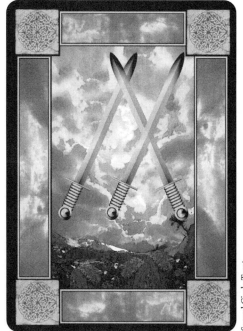

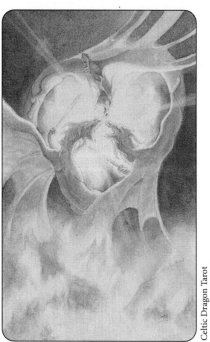

Three of Swords

Pulling the Three of Swords is a disheartening experience in any reading, but in a request for advice, it seems quite perplexing. However, this card too can be a teacher with wisdom to offer. The Three of Swords encourages us to confront and examine our disappointments in order to learn from them and, ultimately, to be able to let them go.

Numerologically, Threes represent self-expression. This card advises the expression of sorrow. Confronting psychological pain and anger is a part of the healing process that is fundamental to many popular therapies. For example, family therapist John Bradshaw urges the need to confide shame, grieve for unmet developmental needs, and do "original pain" work as a prerequisite for healing the inner child and doing ego reconstruction. He suggests that this be done with the help of friends or through therapists because, "You cannot grieve alone, you need someone that legitimizes and validates your pain" (*Homecoming*, pp. 66–80).

If you decide to confront pain, anger, and other negative feelings as a way of dealing with the Three of Swords (interpreted as advice), do so in a protected space. Visit a therapist or confide your problems to a friend (having warned that friend in advance that you need a shoulder to cry on). If you feel that you can summon and examine your feelings by yourself, I suggest that you do so while taking a two-mile walk. For an average person walking briskly, this will take about forty minutes and burn two hundred calories. As you walk along, think about the incidents that have hurt, angered, or worried you, or whatever other fears or conditions may have bothered you. As you bring them up, you may become very agitated and your mind may start replaying these things with increasing intensity. That's okay; don't worry about controlling your emotions right now, but do keep walking. By taking your painful thoughts out into the open, they will be dissipated into nature and metabolized by the spirits of Fire, Earth, Air, and Water, who can well transform these energies. The physical stress that may be aroused will be dispersed by this physical exertion. Two miles of this should be enough to fulfill the exercise in emotion that the Three of Swords calls for, so satisfy yourself that when the walk is over, it's over, and the card's conditions have been met. If you can't shut the emotions off, keep walking until they shut off by themselves—which they will do within a reasonable period of time.

Going to the heart of a matter may require a laserlike focus on the nucleus, the source of mental pain. Calm your mind enough to identify just what it is that's giving you grief. Issues may be confused, but be patient and listen to your intuition. When you identify a core issue, you will usually experience a sense of recognition, and even of relief. For especially effective techniques for dealing with uncomfortable issues, refer to Eugene T. Gendlin's book, *Focusing*, which teaches how to use your somatic senses to get at the source of problems through a shift, or series of shifts, in awareness.

In line with the Three cards' emphasis on creative solutions: artists, musicians, and writers have often used the experience of pain to inform their work, so consider how you might draw inspiration from whatever troubled situations you are dealing with.

This card's advice to confront painful issues may especially apply if you have questions about your health, as it has been recognized that suppression of turbulent feelings can provoke illness. In some very specific medical contexts, the Three of Swords may suggest that surgery is needed, while the reversed card may advise against it.

Since reversed cards suggest dealing with issues in ways that are more low-key, the Three of Swords reversed could advise you to deal with personal pain by acknowledging it but keeping it to yourself—especially if you are in a situation where it would be inappropriate to express it, or where it would create too much of a burden for other loved ones who are dealing with their own pain. It may also suggest a need to get beyond personal pain: get it out, confront it, examine it, and then get over it. Your ego state is surely a major contributor to the pain you experience when dealing with the Three of Swords, so getting over it may require you to let go of some ego needs. In her workbook for use with the alternative Tarot deck *Motherpeace*, Vicki Noble touches on this, discussing how this reversed card indicates "giving up some of the soap opera tactics of ego involvement and mental judging" (p. 5). This reminds me of a saying I read somewhere: "There is no such thing as a dark night of the soul, only a dark night of the ego."

A distancing from pain can be achieved when we understand how our thoughts affect our reality. Anyone who has experienced chronic depression (as opposed to those whose depression is brought on by some cataclysmic event) has some insight into the malleability of reality. When you come out of a depressive episode, you recognize that nothing in your external reality has changed: there is as much or as little money in the bank as there ever was, the house is as clean or as messy as it ever was, and so on. What depression does change, however, is our perception of our conditions: things look so much bleaker and impossible to deal with when we're in the throes of depression. The Swords cards deal with the way we approach reality, and this knowledge can empower us to take control of our perceptions and thereby change our moods and attitudes.

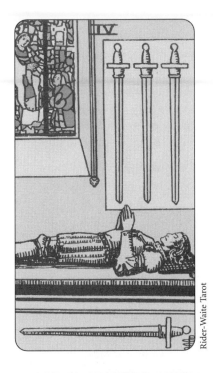
Rider–Waite Tarot

four
of
Swords

Sacred Circle Tarot

Witches Tarot

four of Swords

The cards in the Tarot suits often tend to be linked in sequence, so the Four of Swords may refer to the need to recover from a wounding, that wounding being depicted in the previous card, which is often portrayed as three swords piercing a heart. If not a wounding, then at least the experience of a major frustration is implied in the Four of Swords. You may feel that you can't move, that you're paralyzed because you're being attacked, or at least confounded, by strife and conflict from all four directions. Under these circumstances, the best course of action may simply be to bide time. If you can find a place to retreat to for rest and recuperation, all the better. The Four of Swords' advice relates to its popular image depicting a knight, or the effigy of a knight, in seclusion and repose.

As a card of general advice, the Four of Swords can be broadly applied, calling for the need to contain conflict in your life and find a time and place for rest and relaxation. If you have sought advice for dealing with difficult people or other types of problems, this card suggests avoiding them. Here, retreat from problems is not an act of cowardice or an abnegation of responsibility, but a recognized need for self-renewal. A certain time factor is indicated: "Time heals all wounds," but the Four of Swords does not suggest a quick recovery. Obviously, the need for retreat indicates that this would not be the best time to get involved in new activities, enterprises, relationships, etc.

For busy, overworked people, this card suggests a period of enforced restraint. If you are the kind of person who can't stay away from competition and contention (perhaps a "Type A" personality), this card urges you to get tough on yourself and enforce your own restraints before something like a breakdown in health takes this matter out of your own hands. A retreat can renew you emotionally, physically, and spiritually—and enable you to gain new insight and creative inspiration. For people who are not accustomed to demanding private space and time alone, the solitude and going inward implied here can be scary, but it can also produce revelations. The Four of Swords can also represent a mental retreat. Sometimes, getting far enough away from an issue allows you to regain your perspective and focus.

While you are seeking a place of rest, make sure your personal boundaries are respected and protected. Since the symbolism of four often refers to enclosures, to physical spaces, the Four of Swords advises retreating to a private place, known as a *regenerative space*. It may also indicate a need for a safe space, which is an emotionally supportive environment, as well as a special state of mind. Find a place among people with whom you can be yourself and express your feelings without fear of ridicule or criticism, and make it known through your words and actions that other people are in a safe space when they are in your presence. If you have been agitating conditions in your own home and family (possibly due to a need to dominate the situation), there is now a need to restore peace and purify the space so that it can become a house of healing. Part of this process may require leaving the home and retreating to some other healing space so you can return with new clarity and perspective.

When the Four of Swords comes up reversed, the Tarot may suggest that although you need time for rest and regeneration, you should not stay too long away from life's necessary and unavoidable challenges, from the realms of action and ideas. Emerge from your solitude and shift your focus from the inner life back to the things of the world.

five
of
Swords

FIVE

five of Swords

Illustrations of the Five of Swords commonly show a man in the foreground clutching three swords and looking disdainfully back toward two hunched and defeated-looking figures. Two swords lie on the ground, as if the other two people had dropped them in defeat. And, in fact, the Thoth deck labels this card "Defeat." In an ordinary Tarot reading done for insight or prediction, the central figure in a card tends to show what the subject/querent is up against, and so the Five of Swords can imply that he or she is headed for a downfall. The defeat and disaster suggested by the Five of Swords could relate to the idea that in the contentious Swords suit, the Five's restless energy, the desire to press for change, and the impulse to self-assertion and adventurism can compel a person to stir up trouble, which can bring a host of humiliating problems down on him- or herself.

In a reading for advice, however, a card is interpreted as suggesting some sort of action a person can take, or a quality of energy to channel, in order to deal with the situation in question. Therefore, the advice interpretations in this book tend to take card illustrations somewhat literally, suggesting that you can identify with and model the central figure in a card. In the case of the Five of Swords, this enables us to go with the more positive symbolism of both Swords and Fives, reading it as indicating a need to assert oneself in order to bring about change. This presupposes a need to break away from confining circumstances.

The Five cards call us out of our settled and complacent situations to take on challenges, so the Five of Swords may suggest entry into the realm of conflict. This card urges you to get involved in the matter in question, especially with struggles in the larger world and with groups of people. A competitive, take-charge attitude is appropriate here. If you are lucky enough to have had some of the regenerative time and space suggested in the Four of Swords, you can enter the struggle in a superior position, with renewed strength and clarity. Bear in mind that Five cards represent stimulation, sensation-seeking, expansion, and opportunity, so you can emulate this card by adjusting your attitude to take pleasure in the changes and challenges that life's difficulties present. You might further actualize this card by putting yourself through tests of skill and endurance, and engaging in friendly competition, whether in some sport, intellectual contest, or other activity—mindful that what's important is not whether you win or lose, but the experience you get in playing the game.

Most of us do, of course, prefer to have the upper hand in any situation, though Tarot artists' nuances often add a somewhat disapproving tone to this card. There are situations in which self-assertion is necessary, even if that runs contrary to your nature or to other peoples' desires or plans. For example, you may have to step in and take charge of a situation just to get something done. Self-assertion may also be necessary if you have long been subordinating your needs, beliefs, and personal expression to accommodate other people, especially if their treatment has involved belittlement and criticism. Of course, this does not mean that you have to turn the tables, becoming cruel and tyrannical yourself. However, the people you deal with may have extreme reactions if you have never spoken up for yourself before. You may encounter narcissistic rage: people who don't recognize other peoples' boundaries can act first with disbelief, then outrage, when someone says "no" to them.

The type of self-assertion associated with the Five of Swords may also be of an intellectual or ideological nature, as the Swords cards are very mentally oriented, dealing with ideas and mindsets. Many numerologists attribute the number five to the planet Mercury, which represents our mental processes and corresponds to a god archetype who delighted in the use of wit as well as trickery. To apply all of this as general advice for common situations, this could be seen as a call for creative problem solving. Deal with difficult people or situations by viewing the problem from different angles. The presence of this card suggests that you need to step outside of your normal conceptual framework to gain a new understanding of the matter, as well as of the mindsets of other people involved.

In *Spitirual Tarot*, Echols and her coauthors propose some alternative interpretations of the Five of Swords. In a reinterpretation of the usual image of domination or defeat, they suggest that the central figure could show resourcefulness by "picking up what others have discarded and profiting by it" (p. 153). This can be read as advice, relating to the problem-solving approach and the opportunism associated with the number five.

The reversed Five of Swords can represent someone who is in a dominant position, but yields or relaxes his or her control for a purpose. When you draw the reversed Five of Swords in an advice reading, it may suggest that in order to bring about change, you must make yourself vulnerable or give up a position of advantage. Let go of the need to be the winner, or to be right, or to have the last word, or to be the one in charge. This is not something that most of us care to do, but the Tarot may see certain greater advantages to be gained. Perhaps your insistence that the people you deal with accept a certain idea or a certain way of doing things has created hostility, driven people away from you, and thrown barriers up to harmonious interaction. Relaxing your demands and accepting other peoples' suggestions or criticism may demonstrate that you can be flexible and easier to work and live with.

Six of Swords

SWORDS 6 SWORDS

Earned Success

Six of Swords

The Six of Swords represents the sort of respite from conflict that enables us to put our minds to constructive purposes. As a card of general advice, the Six of Swords recommends that we create a peaceful interlude by setting conflicts aside or looking for ways to get away from daily stress—perhaps through travel or retreat. This card is in favor of plans to move or travel, and would especially advise taking opportunities that enable you to live or work in a safer, more peaceful place.

One of the best ways to refresh the mind and get away from stress and struggle is to take off and go somewhere. This may be one reason why many decks associate this card with travel and portray a figure or figures in a boat, sailing away toward another shore. The experience of dislocation allows us to learn new things, and often prompts new and startling insights into our issues and problems. It enables us to return refreshed, with the clarity to implement new strategies for dealing with our daily struggles. Dislocation is especially recommended if you have been dealing with creative block or some type of puzzle or problem that needs to be worked out. It also effects a transitional state that can have an amazing influence in curing health problems and helping individuals to break with bad habits and other troublesome behavior patterns.

The quiet intervals denoted by the Six of Swords are good times to plan activities that promote good will and understanding between individuals, factions, or communities that are potentially adversarial. For people who are engaged in a dispute, this card suggests coming together in a neutral space, a place set aside, where it is understood that differences are to be worked out in a friendly and creative manner. The focus should be on dealing with the facts, facing them in a scientific and dispassionate manner.

On the other hand, there may be some cases where this card would recommend getting out of a situation, emulating the pictured image of a boat sailing away. If you are in a very bad situation, such as a nasty conflict that appears to be a no-win situation—look for a way out. There's nothing ignoble about retreat. Cut your losses. Get out while the getting is good.

The Swords are cards of conflict as well as intellectual challenge, while the Sixes can denote time set aside for artistic and aesthetic pursuits. Thus, this card suggests that you channel your frustration, rage, and other conflicted energies into some form of creative work that engages the mind as well as the senses.

As advice, the reversed Six of Swords tends to recommend less abrupt displacements than the upright card. Perhaps a simple "time out" is all that is required.

This card's reversed occurrence may also denote a situation in which you can't get away to find the relief you need, so you must find some way to bring relief to you. If you must, try to take a psychological vacation through escapist pleasures that are available to you, and practice meditative techniques that enable you to maintain clarity and a peaceful space, even if struggles and power plays are going on around you. Maintain a safe and neutral space about you, an island of refuge, for the well-being of others too.

Seven
of
Swords

Rider-Waite Tarot

SWORDS (7) SWORDS

Unstable Effort

Golden Dawn Tarot

Celtic Dragon Tarot

Seven of Swords

In the Seven of Swords, the mental clarity of the Swords suit combined with the inventive powers of Seven denotes the ability to see how things work, to understand other peoples' mental processes, to penetrate (as well as to use) illusion, and to predict chains of consequence that stretch into the future. As general advice, this card suggests anticipating problems and taking preemptive actions. In all cases, you must act with future consequences in mind. Get the information you need, then act quickly, calmly, and confidently. The popular illustration of this card, which shows a man stealing away with some swords, reflects this action orientation.

With the Sevens, there is often an element of the unexpected. The man pictured in this card seems to be using deception and illusion (an attribute of the number seven) to advantage. In fact, this card's qualities and its central figure call to mind the Greek hero Odysseus. He was the mastermind behind the Trojan Horse, and was a man of *metis*, a word for skill and cunning, which was much admired by the ancient Greeks. You can use this card as inspiration to come up with unique, even off-the-wall, solutions or approaches to problems. If you have to deal with adversaries, competitors, or problem people, do something they do not expect. Of course, this means that you have to break with your own behavior patterns and habits of thought, which takes some doing, since most of us tend to be blind to these things.

In order to form new and unconventional plans of action and depart from your normal patterns—for whatever purpose, whether to deal with problems, to generate new ideas, or to help you change the future—consider looking into your shadow, which consists of interests, abilities, and character traits that you have suppressed or left undeveloped. It may be that some neglected or forgotten trait is just the thing you need for your coping strategy.

It is important, here, to point out that the shadow doesn't consist of only bad things, and a trait that is undesirable under one sort of circumstances may be appropriate in another. For example, a very courteous person would have rudeness in his or her shadow, but there may be some situations, such as in dealing with obnoxious people, where rudeness is warranted. Traits that we normally consider positive can also be in the shadow, as in the case of suppressed qualities of leadership in a shy person. In some artists' renditions of the Seven of Swords, the man pictured carrying off the swords is a rather sneaky looking fellow, and this evokes some disapproval because cunning is a shadow trait in our society. However, who is to say that he doesn't have a good reason for carrying off those swords?

The more negative expression of the Seven of Swords is a state of paranoia, where one is always planning for the worst, and is distrustful of others, reading sinister meanings into their actions. People who act from this state are thinking, "I'm going to screw you before you can get a chance to screw me." If the Seven of Swords presents itself reversed in an advice reading, it may indicate that this could be a problem, and suggests that you be a little more relaxed and trusting. If you have certain contracts or arrangements with people, take all the necessary and usual precautions, but don't allow distrust to sabotage the relationships. Practice the golden rule, and give others the benefit of the doubt until given solid reasons to do otherwise.

The reversed Seven of Swords may also advise against the sort of convoluted thinking that results in self-sabotage. Sometimes, trying to plan and anticipate actions too far into the future can trip us up. This reversed card suggests making reasonable plans and predictions, but being flexible enough to go with the flow or adjust to other outcomes when situations change.

Rider-Waite Tarot

Eight
of
Swords

EIGHT OF SWORDS

GUENEVERE
AT THE STAKE

Legend Tarot

SWORDS (8) SWORDS

Shortened Force

Golden Dawn Tarot

Eight of Swords

The solidity and stability symbolized by the number eight (the balanced arrangement of two squares) can represent blockage and inability to move. When in the realm of conflict that the Swords cards represent, this can denote paralysis and indecision as a result of trying to sort out too many competing issues. This is graphically portrayed in versions of this card that show a woman in bonds surrounded by eight swords that have been driven into the ground. However, this is another case where a card that is normally bad news takes on a neutral interpretation as a card of advice. As a suggested course of action, this card tends to have two general applications: it suggests avoiding action or imposing some sort of restraint on the Self.

Depending on the nature of your question, this card could advise you against taking action or getting involved in a new matter, or to avoid making decisions or choices. This is not the time to make a move or start something new. However, in keeping with the card's symbolism of binding obligations, it suggests that you stick with those projects and enterprises in which you are already involved, and that you honor existing commitments and contracts.

This card may simply call for restraint in the very general sense of the term, as in acting with restraint, or practicing self-restraint with regard to some matter. It may also require you to impose special restrictions on yourself, or place yourself in a situation that will force you to stay in one place, keep you out of trouble, or give you an excuse for staying out of entanglement or conflict. Ways to take up this advice could include committing yourself to a contract, job, study program, or volunteer activity, or planning a very tight schedule of activities in order to avoid going somewhere or being drawn into an activity that you have reasons for wanting to stay out of. This may be especially useful advice for people caught between warring factions of family or social groups. You might think about what kind of excuses you can bind yourself with if you're concerned about getting drawn into problems. If other people pressure you to get involved, tell them, "I'm all tied up."

If you've come into some money, you might put it into long-term accounts or other investments where it will be tied up, so you won't be tempted to blow it right away, or so that others won't be able to impose on you to lend it to them.

If you have approached the Tarot about health concerns, this card may advise placing yourself on a restrictive dietary regime, or caution you to restrict certain activities.

For people seeking to solve a problem, Mary K. Greer has a unique take on this card, which can be applicable to advice readings: she suggests in her book *Tarot Constellations* that the Eight of Swords can represent a situation in which, "You deliberately get yourself in an apparently impossible situation in order to force a really creative solution" (p. 122).

Reversed, the Eight of Swords might suggest that you need to start loosening bonds and extricating yourself from a confining situation. Do so in a cautious and conscientious manner, with attention to details. Try to detach yourself mentally and emotionally so you can analyze the tangle of issues you have to deal with. This relates to Gail Fairfield's keyword for this card, which is "Organizing Thoughts."

Nine
of
Swords

NINE OF SWORDS

LILY MAID
OF ASTOLAT

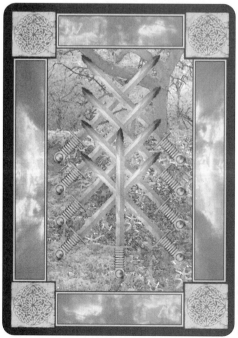

Nine of Swords

The Nine of Swords, which commonly depicts a lone woman in bed crying, is one card we're never happy to see, but as a card of advice, it calls us to examine our fears and anxieties, and any other emotional and mental states that keep us up at night. Some worries are legitimate, and some are not, so you must consider the following advice alternatives in the context of what you know to be true of your own situation.

In an advice reading, the appearance of the Nine of Swords can call your attention to something that you should indeed worry about. It may mean that the situation you are dealing with is more serious than you think. This does not necessarily mean that things are headed for disaster, just that the matter requires some extra thought and attention from you. If you have free-floating anxieties, but don't know their source, try meditative and focusing techniques. It may be that there is something at the back of consciousness, nagging to make itself known (similar to the sort of nagging feeling you may have if you forget that you've left the oven or iron on). To find out more about the nature of the problem, you can look to the other cards in the spread, or do another Tarot reading to request clarification. When you are dealing with a known problem, you should investigate the matter in question more deeply, make contingency plans for other problems that might develop, and do anything else you can to make things better. Try to break your problem down into smaller components, or spend your time working around the edges of it. Some of our greatest worries come from a lack of knowledge about what is actually going on, and from a lack of preparation. You may find that your mind will be greatly set at ease just by having more information, and by having a plan.

On the other hand, many worries are counterproductive, so if you have already done everything you can about a certain situation, but your worries still keep running through your head in a sort of cybernetic loop, one effective way to confront them is to construct worst-case scenarios. Ask yourself, "What is the worst thing that could happen?" (Barring the sort of bizarre catastrophes that none of us can do anything about, such as dirigible accidents, supernova explosions, anvils falling out of the sky, etc.). Then ask, "What is the worst thing that is actually likely to happen?" You'll find that the worst thing that could happen is seldom the worst thing that is likely to happen. Furthermore, both the worst thing that could happen and the worst thing that is likely to happen, however painful, are usually things that can be managed, and that will diminish with the passage of time. The act of formulating worst-case scenarios does not involve negative thinking if it is done in a calm and objective state of mind. It is a tool for gaining perspective, and can actually boost your optimism and help you manage challenges.

Since the Nine of Swords often deals with criticism turned inward, there may also be a situation in which you need to be a bit more self-critical. Perhaps you've been blaming problems on everything and everyone else, and you need to take a sharper look at your own attitudes and actions.

When you draw the reversed Nine of Swords in an advice reading, the Tarot may be suggesting that you need to detach from your worries and self-criticism so that you can deal with them more objectively. For example, while examining your personal torments, ask yourself whether they come from self-castigation—that is, if you are torturing yourself over hurtful, embarrassing, and other regrettable things you have done. Consider whether the punishment actually fits the crime. Sometimes guilt puts us through suffering that is way out of proportion to the original offense. Ask yourself what level of punishment you would assign to someone else who had done the same thing. If you've already put yourself through more mental punishment than that (and assuming that you've also taken steps, where possible, to try to make things right), then consider the slate as having been cleared.

The reversed Nine of Swords may also advise us to speak out about our worries. While we all know people who are whiners and complainers, we also know people who keep their concerns too much to themselves and put on brave faces out of a sense of politeness or a reluctance to open up to others. If the latter is true for you, be frank about the things that are bothering you, and voice your personal pain and concerns to others. Sometimes it's necessary to have these feelings validated, to be recognized and understood. As the poet Rilke says, ". . . those in need have to step forward, have to say: I am blind, or: I'm about to go blind, or: nothing is going well with me, or: I have a child who is sick, or: right there I'm sort of glued together. . . . They have to sing [i.e., express themselves]; if they didn't sing, everyone would walk past, as if they were fences or trees" (*Selected Poems*, p. 111). Taking further inspiration from Rilke, you might want to try your hand at expressing your feelings in poetry, or in some other creative form. Don't allow yourself to become isolated, and bring enough people into your emotional support system so that you don't need to unburden all of your woes on one person.

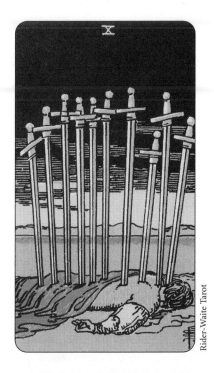

Rider-Waite Tarot

Ten
of
Swords

Sacred Circle Tarot

TEN

Witches Tarot

Ten of Swords

The Ten of Swords, which frequently portrays a body pierced with blades, can represent a lifetime's accumulation of problems and the attitude, for people who are always getting into conflicts, that trouble is a way of life. However, in an advice reading, this card suggests that you consciously confront problems and take on troubles in service to a higher purpose. There are several ways this may apply.

The Ten of Swords may pertain to situations in which you must consciously increase your stress load. It may be necessary to submit to something, such as a hateful job that imposes enormous hardships as well as mental and physical strain, because it is necessary (at least for the time being) for accomplishing a goal. Aspects of your personal life may also have to be sacrificed in service to a goal or cause.

If you have approached the Tarot about people problems, such as in vicious family conflicts, legal tangles, or the accumulation of other types of enemies, this card may advise giving in to them. Sometimes the only way to end a cycle of conflict is to turn the other cheek. Even if you feel that you're in the right, that indeed you're the victim of a great injustice, you may decide that it's better to sacrifice some of your own interests and let the other side have the last word or whatever else it wants, just to restore peace and get out of that loop. For questions pertaining to concerns about loved ones, the Tarot advises that you put up with some hardships or make sacrifices for their sakes.

The ideological nature of the Swords suit indicates that you may have to take some flak for your personal beliefs. There may also be a situation where the Tarot advises you to take a stand in a conflict, in the face of probable loss, on the ideal that it's better to go down with the good guys, even if they're outnumbered.

The Ten of Swords may also suggest that you deal with problems that have been carried forward from the past. One way to do this is to take responsibility for past misdeeds. If you have done something wrong or gotten into some type of trouble, accept the consequences, even if punishment is involved. Accepting consequences is another way to end a downward cycle and begin anew, even if it means starting over with a certain stigma.

When the Ten of Swords is reversed, the Tarot may be telling you that you need to be more selective about what you're willing to put up with. Decide which types of sacrifices and hardships are meaningful and necessary in terms of fulfilling greater purposes. The expression, "Is this the hill you want to die on?"* may also

* This reference comes from Ernest Hemingway's book, *For Whom the Bell Tolls*, p. 336.

be applicable here, referring to the need to decide which conflicts are worth getting involved in.

The reversed Ten of Swords may also come up when you have experienced a crisis in consciousness, brought on by the recognition that self-defeating behaviors and past associations are clinging to your back, trying to drag you down. In this case, the card suggests that you work at breaking old patterns in a systematic manner.

Page
of
Swords

Rider–Waite Tarot

Celtic Dragon Tarot

Sacred Circle Tarot

Page of Swords

Pages try to make sense out of their world, and for the Page of Swords, this amounts to processing a lot of information, sorting out facts, and sizing up people. This Page is especially concerned with studying and negotiating the webs of power relationships that interconnect family, society, and culture. He perceives the locus of power and assesses the relative strengths and weaknesses of others (hence this card is associated in some interpretive systems with spying), and may use this knowledge to manipulate. He is in the process of discerning and defining personal boundaries, both his and other peoples'.

Generally, the appearance of the Page of Swords in an advice reading signals the need to be well informed about things that are going on around you, so it is probably wise not to get involved in new ventures or major commitments at this time unless you're considering a course of study or internship situation. Indications are that the situation at hand will have a major impact on you, but it's still unfolding, so keep your eyes and ears open. Ask questions, and ask again if you don't understand or if you suspect you haven't been given all of the information you need. Don't be afraid to approach older or more powerful people in an effort to keep abreast of what is happening.

Pages can relate to our child ego states, to the child within, and the Page of Swords especially corresponds to what in Transactional Analysis is known as "the little professor" aspect of the child ego state (James and Jongeward, *Born to Win*, pp. 149–52). This is the attentive, intuitive, problem-solving personality within children that prompts them to seek ways to operate on their environment and on the people and things around them. In an advice reading, this may indicate a need to study your situation and then find inventive ways of dealing with it.

This card also recommends that you use tools of communication, such as letter writing, journal keeping, conversations with others, and so on, to define the issue in question and outline your personal position on it.

Page of Swords children are very perceptive and can see through the hypocrisy of the adult world. Sometimes the recognition of early injustices can result in an internalized child who has a lot of cynicism and rage, and has had to learn manipulative ways as a survival skill. If this describes you, when the Page of Swords card comes up reversed, it may be a problem for you. You are advised to resist the tendency to judge people. Refocus your powers of observation to realign your beliefs; look for the good in people and turn toward all things positive.

The reversed Page of Swords may also indicate a need to return to and rethink a matter in question, then apply creative problem solving. Perhaps there is a key to your situation that you have missed. You may need to approach the problem from different angles, using unorthodox methods of seeing and understanding, such as different types of visualization and other imaginative techniques. This may include standing outside of yourself and detaching from your feelings and your normal way of reacting to people and things.

Rider-Waite Tarot

Knight
of
Swords

THE PRINCE OF SWORDS

Witches Tarot

Celtic Dragon Tarot

Knight of Swords

When the Knight of Swords comes up in an advice reading, the Tarot is telling you that you need to be your own advocate. You are urged to take a stand on an idea or cause that's important to you, or on an issue or situation that has a major impact on your life. To do this, you need to adopt the Knight of Swords' mode of action: he is agile, aggressive, and swift to think and act. He is very discerning, and his penetrating intellect gives him what we might call a good bullshit detector. Despite the Knight's appearance, it's important to remember that he doesn't necessarily represent force and violence (although this interpretation may apply within certain contexts) as much as aggressive intellect. Of course, when we do go to battle in our society, it is usually less through physical means than through the mechanisms of the law. As you might expect, the Swords court cards have a lot to do with advocacy and legal contests.

Generally, the Knight of Swords card advocates action and involvement. This card advises you to take timely action to intervene in a crisis. This is not a time for doubt or hesitation. Don't wait around in the hopes that someone else will do the job. The situation calls for you to act quickly to halt or undo some form of damage. Call on the Knight's powers to cut through fear and indecision. The Knight of Swords is also a truth-teller and will speak out against injustice, so this card advises you to tell the truth and let the chips fall where they may.

This card may also signify a need to confront someone regarding the matter in question. You should arm yourself by being well prepared, so have all of your facts straight. This confrontation may also require having all of your paperwork in order. Here, it is important to be prepared to define and defend your personal boundaries. You can more easily deal with the conflicts that arise if you are firm about what you are willing to put up with and what you are not, what is acceptable in your life and what is not, and then stand up for your rights.

Knight of Swords types are good fighters, but because they can also be good communicators, they may be drawn into contested situations in which they find themselves in the position of a negotiator or go-between. If this is the case with you, summon clarity of mind and insight so that you can find some common ground, areas of agreement that enable you to bring contending parties together on important issues.

Although this Knight urges action and involvement, if this card comes up in regard to a question about starting or maintaining a relationship or other long-term commitment, the Tarot's advice on this matter is negative: due to the need for mobility and the prospect of conflict, the focus, at this time, is not on matters of the heart and feelings. In the words of Kipling, "He travels fastest who travels alone." However, the Knight of Swords card may suggest finding a comrade who is an active, stimulating person who can get you involved in causes where you can act on your beliefs, or organizations and activities that provide mental challenges.

The Knights cards have a special function in showing movement toward or away from things, so take note of any adjacent card in whose direction your Knight of Swords is heading (different decks portray him differently). This may give you more specific information about a challenge you are encouraged to take on.

Reversed, this card calls for you to maintain calm detachment and wait to act. Although your warrior energy and survival senses are important here, there may be a need to achieve clarity or to allow other events to sort themselves out. Remember the words of the Tao-te Ching, which says, ". . . those who are good at battle do not become angry, those who are good at prevailing over opponents do not get involved."*

There are certain personality types for whom being "the winner" is all important. If this is causing problems for you by creating barriers to community and intimacy, the reversed Knight of Swords may suggest using the Knight's mental skills to give yourself an attitude adjustment. You have to make a decision that making and preserving relationships and upholding other human values are more important than winning imaginary contests.

* As quoted in the introduction to *The Art of War* by Sun Tzu (Thomas Cleary trans.)

Queen of Swords

QUEEN of SWORDS

THE QUEEN OF SWORDS

Queen of Swords

If the Queen of Swords comes up in an advice reading, you should consider adopting the tough-minded, no-nonsense attitude of this archetype in order to deal with the matter in question. The Queen of Swords speaks her mind and insists that her wisdom and personal power be honored. She has no patience for trivial matters and concerns, and does not see why problems should even exist. She develops skillful means, which are strategies for engineering daily life, so that she can maintain clarity and keep a balance between outer demands and the life of the spirit.

As with all Queen (and King) cards, the Queen of Swords urges you to take on responsibilities and challenges and to assert your personal power. However, if you have drawn this card in response to a question about relationships, it indicates that you should not become involved in or stay in any situation that does not give you mental stimulation or honor your personal autonomy. It also indicates a need to practice "tough love" in relationships.

This card in an advice reading also suggests that you approach a Queen of Swords type of person for help with the matter in question. Seek a mentor in a person who understands and supports your needs for intellectual challenge and expansion, or emulate this quality by recognizing and promoting the ideas and accomplishments of others. When you need an intelligent critic, the Queen of Swords can give you insightful feedback. She excels in assessing thinking processes, and can help you detect flaws in your logic. By teaching you to exercise clear thinking, she shows you how to access your power nature.

When the Queen of Swords comes up reversed in an advice reading, the Tarot suggests that you tone down your personal intensity. Queen of Swords personalities can frustrate people by failing to respond to feelings and concerns. In conversation, these types may be thinking ahead about the things they're going to say next instead of listening to what the other person is saying. This reversed card may be letting you know that it's necessary to open yourself up to others, to attune to them heart-to-heart so you can truly hear them. You can maintain your Queen of Swords intellectual curiosity by probing their thoughts and helping them achieve clarity on their position.

The reversed Queen of Swords may also advise you to deal with a situation by making peace, harmony, and loving relationships a bigger priority. Perhaps your intellectual intensity and passionate dedication to issues alienates people. Cultivate the ability to be relaxed and put people at ease through small talk and other social pleasantries. Give positive strokes by using your special insight to make sincere compliments based on a genuine knowledge of the person. In this way, you provide emotional and spiritual nourishment, which is a form of blessing.

King
of
Swords

King of Swords

When you draw the King of Swords in an advice reading, the Tarot urges you to make a command decision. You may be in a situation where it's up to you, and you alone, to decide what needs to be done next. You are urged to assume a position of leadership, even if it requires that you take on unprecedented hardship, self-discipline, and responsibility. You may even need to be tough-minded and assert your power in a way that is normally distasteful to you.

You can best realize the self-empowerment needed by emulating the King of Swords, who uses knowledge and action effectively to get things done. He considers many different courses of action and sees complex webs of relationships and chains of consequences leading far into the future. The King of Swords often has zero tolerance for human folly and shortcomings, which can make this type of personality hard to get along with. However, the card may here advise that you adopt this no-nonsense mode of thought, perhaps as protection against some trouble or deception that is coming your way. If you are in an adversarial situation, remember that information is power. If dealing with difficult people, be firm but objective and fair-minded. If drawn into a conflict between two or more individuals, there is a need to listen well and to sift the truth from a lot of hysterical meanderings.

The appearance of the King of Swords also suggests that you seek guidance from someone who possesses the above qualities. As a mentor, the King of Swords can be a teacher who challenges you intellectually. Be prepared to take his constructive criticism; don't allow your feelings to block your objectivity. The King of Swords will encourage you to have confidence in your own ideas and to assert them, where appropriate, to assume your rightful position in the world. Also, if you need help with some matter, especially if you have to deal with bureaucracy or an organization, try to identify the person who is actually empowered to do something, and approach him or her directly.

Because he believes Nietzsche's dictum that, "That which does not kill us makes us stronger," the King of Swords type is likely to impose hardships or unpleasant learning experiences on his loved ones and subordinates "for their own good," without perceiving that not all individuals are of types that can benefit from such experiences. Thus, when this card comes up reversed, the Tarot may be hinting that you need to accommodate individual differences. Remember that a stimulating challenge for one person can be a motivation killer for another. Be willing to try different strategies to meet different peoples' growth needs.

The reversed card may also suggest letting go of the need to control a situation or to insist on confronting people with facts or reality. This is a situation where it is more important to promote harmony and good will than to be frank or to see that things are done in a certain way.

Appendix I: About the Tarot

The following information is extracted from my book, *Tarot Spells*, with some additions and modifications, to provide a brief overview of the history and use of the Tarot.

The Tarot is a series of cards, in some ways similar to playing cards, that is best known for its use in fortunetelling. Tarot decks generally take the form of a pack of seventy-eight cards. Twenty-two cards make up the Major Arcana, the more esoteric segment of the Tarot, which contains familiar cards like the Fool, the Hanged Man, the High Priestess, and so on. The symbolic pictures of these cards depict the individual's journey through life, in which he or she undergoes life's lessons to gain experience and achieve self-actualization. The other fifty-six cards, known as the Minor Arcana, are divided into suits (similar to those of playing cards) of fourteen cards each, including the court cards: Kings, Queens, Knights, and Pages. In some decks, the minor cards are illustrated with pictures of people in different situations, while other decks have only the symbols of their suits: the Pentacles, Wands, Cups, Swords, and their variations.

The exact origin of the Tarot is uncertain. Scholars who have probed this subject point to the fourteenth and fifteenth centuries as the earliest time during which the existence of the Tarot as we know it can be proven. Eden Gray, author of one of the most popular Tarot textbooks, cites A.D. 1390 as the date of some Tarot cards displayed in a European museum. However, like many other scholars, Gray felt that this particular pack had more ancient antecedents.

The older versions of the Tarot have in their graphics and symbolism a strong medieval Italian influence, so some scholars, pointing to correspondences in the art and culture of that period, suggest a medieval Italian origin for the Tarot. However, many admirers of the Tarot feel that it is far more ancient than that. They differ in their opinion of the Tarot's beginnings. In its motifs they see derivations of the mystical traditions of such varied cultures as ancient Egypt, India, China, Korea, Persia, and the Gypsies, as well as Hermetic, Cabalistic, and Albigensian philosophical teachings. Astrological and numerological symbolism has also been projected into the Tarot.

Just as there is dispute over the origin of the Tarot, there are also varying opinions on the meaning of its name. The word Tarot is closely tied to the history of cards (in general) and the design features of cards, for as Stuart Kaplan points out in *Tarot Classic*, the words *tarocchi* and *tarocchino*, which are used in Italian Tarot decks, are also the names of card games; Parisian playing card makers of the late sixteenth century called themselves *Tarotiers*; the word *tarotee* is applied to the criss-cross designs on the back of early cards; and spiral dot patterns on the margins of some playing cards were called *tares*, while the cards featuring such designs were called *tarots* or *tarotees* (p. 32). However, other students of Tarot have suggested more exotic roots for the word. Angeles Arrien cites different theories, including some that assert that (1) the name is derived from the Egyptian *Ta-rosh*, meaning "the royal way"; or (2) it might be related to *rota*, the Latin word for wheel; or (3) it might have Cabalistic associations, related to *Torah*, the word for "the law." She also mentions that the word *tar* means "a deck of cards" in the gypsy language, and derives from the Sanskrit word *taru* (*The Tarot Handbook*, p. 16). Personally, I favor the possible Latin association because the Rota Fortuna is pictured as one of the cards, Fortuna is the goddess-presence behind the Tarot, and the cult of Fortuna had a practice of inscribing fortunes on tablets. However, Tarot may well be one of those words that was shaped and popularized by the confluence of several different traditions, thus making it all the more meaningful.

Although the historical origins and the meaning of the word Tarot cannot be proven, I think we can agree that its motifs are very compelling and correspond to fundamental human psychological experiences. Tarot cards reveal mystical and philosophical truths through their pictures. These symbolic images open the doors of the subconscious by drawing from ancient archetypes found deep within our collective subconscious minds. Because the Tarot's psychic and psychological meanings have such appeal, it is becoming more popular for use in meditation and for other purposes.

Today's artists have found special inspiration in the Tarot imagery, so many new versions of these cards have been designed, and the Tarot's increasing popularity is making it widely available. I feel that those of you who are just getting into Tarot will be pleasantly surprised by the selection available, and that you'll be able to experiment with a number of fascinating decks in your exploration of the magic that is implicit in every card. In recent years, the Tarot has blossomed in many versions from an extremely wide diversity of sources. So many decks are currently available that it would not be practical to mention them all here. Some of them hearken back to the early Renaissance versions, while others take some interesting new directions.

In 1910, Arthur Edward Waite conceived and commissioned a deck that was illustrated by Pamela Colman Smith and printed by the Rider company (therefore sometimes known as the Rider-Smith-Waite deck, or variations thereof). Prior to that, most of the decks were fairly simple and preserved the medieval influences in their stark and sometimes crude images. Waite altered and/or embellished some of the older Tarot images in the Major Arcana, and ascribed detailed illustrations and fixed meanings to the Minor Arcana. Waite's deck became very popular, and his illustrations and interpretations became the standard on which many newer Tarot versions have been based.

For centuries, the Tarot has been used to foresee the patterns of the future. For Tarot readings, the cards are shuffled and then laid out in certain traditional spreads. The future is projected by interpreting the symbols in relation to the questions asked. Similarly, the cards can be shuffled, laid out, and studied to show the individual's place in terms of spiritual development, as well as in the grand scheme of life.

Those of us who value the Tarot for its pertinent and insightful commentary on the state of our lives and future prospects have different ideas as to how and why it works. There are some people who believe that spirits move the cards into position, and others who believe that the cards are meaningfully arranged through some subtle form of telekinesis. Some say that there's no magic in the act of shuffling and laying out the cards, but that we use them, somewhat like Rorschach blots, to arrive at meanings that are relevant to us. A newer explanation, which relates to Jungian ideas of causality, synchronicity, and the collective unconscious, offers that the patterns of Tarot cards and other divinatory systems are meaningful because of the interconnectedness of all things. This is the view that I favor, though I don't discount the possibility that the other factors are at work as well. Before I came around to this point of view, I would not do a Tarot reading if I was not feeling good or psychically attuned because I feared that I could not properly connect with the spirits or with my psychic resources. This attitude shift has enabled me to work with the Tarot more regularly and more readily because the selection of cards is seen as part of a greater pattern, and not dependent on how I feel at a given moment.

Tarot also has unique value as a tool for meditation. By reflecting on the deep meanings of the symbols, the individual can look inward to probe truths about the Self, or look outward to grasp transcendental cosmic knowledge.

Today, the magic of the Tarot is also being enthusiastically explored. Practitioners are developing psychic and psychological exercises to encourage self-knowledge, healing, creativity, etc. Indeed, the Tarot has been worked into systems of High Magick, that is, rituals for higher spiritual transformation. Truly, the use of the Tarot has been expanded from a means of sensing patterns and events to a forthright method to influence our own evolution.

Appendix II:
Rite to Fortuna, Goddess of Tarot

Those of us who work with the Tarot must always be mindful of the spiritual nature of this activity: when we probe the mysteries of time and life, and ponder the diverging strands of possibility, we are in the presence of a goddess.

The name of the goddess who is perhaps best known for her concern with the Tarot and other forms of divination is, of course, the Goddess Fortuna. In some versions of the Tarot, she is the familiar form presiding over the Wheel of Fortune. The Wheel of Fortune was a very popular symbol in medieval and Renaissance art, and is represented as card number ten in Tarot decks. Fortuna's wheel shows that she presides over the cycles of life and change, as well as opportunities, luck, turning points in personal destiny, surprises, and things as yet unknown. In the ancient Etruscan tradition, her statues were often heavily draped, further suggesting her connection with the mysteries.

In classical times, Fortuna had an ancient temple at Praeneste, a city with many Greek and Etruscan influences; her oracle there has been described as "by far the most renowned in Italy" (Fowler, *Religious Experience of the Roman People*, p. 72). Fortuna Praenestina had a yearly festival June 9–11—the Fasti Praenest—where those who sought her advice drew wooden tokens or tablets from a chest. These tablets had prophetic messages inscribed on them, though as these messages were often ambiguous, the individual had to make his or her own interpretations based on his or her own intuition and experience.

It is important to distinguish between the Goddess Fortuna, who represents mutable human fortunes, and inexorable Fate, known to the ancients as Fatum or Ananke. Fortuna and Fate were not considered to be one and the same. Fortuna was generally considered to be a benevolent deity, most commonly pictured with a cornucopia, which reveals that the ancients viewed her primarily as a gracious goddess of abundance, often addressed as Bona Fortuna. As Plutarch said in the *Moralia*, Fortune:

> holds in her hand,
> that renowned horn of plenty,
> not filled full of ever-blooming fruits
> but as much
> as all the earth and all the seas
> and rivers and mines and harbors
> bear,

so much does she pour forth,
in plenty and abundance.

Another holiday in honor of this goddess, known as Fors Fortuna, was on June 24, the date of the summer solstice before some calendar adjustments, and was an especially big and important religious holiday. It was celebrated with family picnics and lots of revelry along the river Tiber, where several of Fortuna's shrines were located. People partied along the banks and sailed up and down the river on boats decorated with flowers. The fact that this big festival and temple dedication coincided with the summer solstice shows that Fortuna has some solar associations, and the Wheel of Fortune may thus also be related to the sun wheel. Goddess-lorist Barbara Walker relates Fortuna to Vortumna, an earlier Etruscan goddess who turned "the celestial wheel of the stars and also the karmic wheel of fate" (*Woman's Encyclopedia*, p. 321), and suggests that "Fortuna-Vortumna personified all the cycles of Time and Being" (*Secrets of Tarot*, p. 94).

There are conflicting beliefs about Fortuna's family relationships: a popular tradition sees her as the daughter of Jupiter (she is called Fortuna Primigenia—the first born), but another tradition represents Fortuna as his mother. Statues show Jupiter and Juno as two small children, sitting in Fortuna's lap. In either case, in her role as gracious goddess of luck and abundance, Fortuna relates to some of the astrological qualities of the planet Jupiter.

In addition to her cornucopia, Fortuna was often pictured carrying a double-sided ship's rudder, symbolizing her power to guide human destinies. Her Greek counterpart, Tyche, had also been portrayed with cornucopia and rudder, as was her later manifestation as Isis Fortuna, when she became a major figure in the romanized cult of Isis. Later depictions of Fortuna sometimes portrayed her as winged, blindfolded (perhaps indicating that she dispenses favors without regard to character), and standing on or next to a ball or sphere (which may symbolize her influence over time and world). As Isis Fortuna, she sometimes wears a lotus crown. The Wheel of Fortune is a symbol that came to be attributed to her later on.

As the goddess of luck and chance, Fortuna has many counterparts. As mentioned, Fortuna's Greek equivalent is the Goddess Tyche, who rules luck and random chance, and intervenes in human destinies. Tyche is sometimes identified with Dike (Justice) to whom dice—originally knucklebones used in divination—are ascribed. In Rome, Fortuna was closely related to Felicitas, another goddess personifying good luck. As Fortuna Praenestina, she has ties to Feronia (the Etruscan Ferentinum), a goddess of fate, wild nature, fertility, and abundance. She is closely identified with the Etruscan Goddess Nortia, who presides over luck, ceremonies, and magic, as well as health and healing, and was a prime deity of the Volsci tribe of Tuscany. Fortuna was one goddess who continued to be popular through Renaissance times, sometimes under different names and personifications, such as the medieval German Frau Saelde.

The word *fortuna* is believed to come from the root word *fero* (alternate form *fors*), and to mean that she is the goddess who "brings" or "brings forth." Her cornucopia also symbolize the idea of bringing forth, as Fortuna brings forth abundance, growth, and emergent plant life (she has agricultural associations related to the desire for healthy crops), children (her worship was popular with women concerned with fertility, safety in childbearing, and interest in their children's destinies), and opportunities, surprises, and things unknown (hence the concern with chance, turning points in destiny, and fortunetelling).

In rune working, Fortune's presence is related to that of the Norns, and there is a certain philosophical parallel between Fortuna, her cornucopia, the idea of "bringing forth," and the rune called *perthro* or *peorth* (ᛈ), which rune lorists suggest may represent a dice cup, an object used for casting lots in gambling and divination. Gamblers hope that Lady Luck will bring them good fortune with games of chance, and divination is always concerned with discerning the surprises that fate brings forth. Certain interpretations also relate *perthro* to the womb of the goddess, and this can be compared to Fortuna's supplicants' concern with bringing forth children and learning their fates. *Peorth* has also been linked to the well of the Norns, and—carrying these associations a little bit further—one can see relationships to the symbolism of the cauldron of the goddess, which contains the roiling and boiling stuff of raw potential from which manifested realities flow forth.

From her long list of interests and associations, we can see that when we work with the Tarot, we are doing Lady Fortune's work.

If you wish to honor and affirm this goddess presence when you consult the Tarot or other divinatory media, whether for prediction or for advice, you can make a small ceremony of it by using the following devotion.

Obtain a candle to dedicate in honor of this goddess as Fortuna, Tyche, and the other goddesses of divination. You can use any color that you associate with this goddess presence, but white is appropriate because it contains all colors of the spectrum, symbolizing all of the strands of possibility that you wish to look into. If you wish, carve the *peorth* rune into the candle. Anoint the candle with fragrant oil; some scents that are believed to be especially appropriate for divination are sandalwood, benzoin, clove, myrrh, bay, orange, lavender, lemongrass, lemon verbena, and peppermint. Add to the ambience by burning incense in one of these scents, too.

Then recite the following words:

Oh Lady Fortune,
I call upon you as Tyche, Dike,
Feronia, Nortia, Vortumna,
Saelde, Felicitas,
Isis Fortuna, Fortuna Praenestina,
and in all of your other names, forms, and manifestations.*
You turn the wheel of Time and Life,
You know the diverging pathways of Destiny,
and the surprises that Life is yet to bring forth.
I honor and acknowledge your gracious Presence,
and respectfully request your help.
Please guide me so that I may advise and interpret wisely.
Fero Fortuna, Fortuna Scribunda!
Fero Fortuna, Imperatrix Mundi!
As I now proceed with this reading,
I honor you, as I do your work.

Proceed with your session. When finished, extinguish the candle, while saying:

Oh far-sighted Goddess,
I thank you for your help and guidance!
Blessed Be!

* If you are aware of other names for this goddess, or feel that she has affinities with other god and goddess presences that you are interested in, you can insert their names into the above rite of calling, modifying the wording where necessary.

265

Appendix III:
The Celtic Cross Spread

On page 14, I mentioned that cards Seven through Nine of the Celtic Cross Tarot spread can be reinterpreted in terms of advice after you have used this spread to gain an overview of your situation. Since I brought up the subject, I may have piqued the curiousity of newcomers who are not familiar with this spread. Therefore, following is a more thorough description of the Celtic Cross method of divination.

The Celtic Cross method of laying out Tarot cards seems to have been around forever, but I learned it back in the early seventies, probably from Arthur Edward Waite's book *The Pictorial Key to the Tarot*, or Eden Gray's book, *The Tarot Revealed*. It is the most popular spread for detailed Tarot readings. Most readers assign very similar meanings to the cards' positions on the cross, although usually with some modifications, as I have also done, as a result of coming under other influences over the years and forming my own habits of thought along the way.

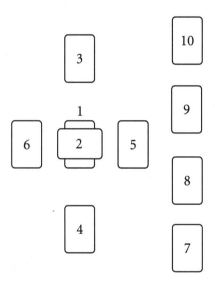

Many readers put a significator card under Card One. I don't always do this, (especially if I'm reading for myself), because I let the Tarot choose Card One as the significator, while simultaneously representing the individual's basic position in the matter in question. If you want to use a significator, pick a card out of the deck that to your mind best represents yourself or the person you are reading for, and lay that card down first.

Card One represents your situation and your state of mind. Card Two shows forces that are working at cross purposes to your desires, or how your desires or intentions may be divided. Card Three represents issues that are below the surface, working on a subconscious level. Card Four shows the influence of the recent past, or of things that you are moving away from. Card Five shows what is uppermost in your mind, often relating to your hoped-for outcome. Card Six shows where things are headed, and what can be expected to manifest in the near future.

Moving to the adjacent configuration of four cards, Card Seven (notice that it's at the bottom of the vertical column) represents the role that you are acting out. Card Eight shows the environmental influences that are acting on you. Card Nine shows your main issue areas, that is, your hopes and fears. Card Ten shows what is likely to result from all of this.

As I mentioned in the section Reading and Intrepreting Tarot Cards for Advice, you can apply advice interpretations to cards Seven through Nine in this spread, depending on how you feel about the outcome card.

Works Cited

Arrien, Angeles. *The Tarot Handbook*. Sonoma, CA: Arcus, 1987.

Auden, W. H. "September 1st, 1939." *Selected Poems*. Edward Mendelson, ed. New York: Random-Vintage, 1979.

Birkhauser-Oeri, Sibylle. *The Mother: Archetypal Image in Fairy Tales*. Michael Mitchell trans. Toronto: Inner City Books, 1988.

Bly, Robert. *Iron John: A Book About Men*. Reading, MA: Addison-Wesley, 1990.

Bolen, Jean Shinoda. *The Tao of Psychology*. San Francisco: Harper & Row, 1979.

Bradshaw, John. *On: The Family*. Audiotape. HCI Audio Books, 1989.

———— *Homecoming: Reclaiming and Championing Your Inner Child*. New York: Bantam, 1990.

Bronner, Simon J. *Grasping Things: Folk Material Culture and Mass Society in America*. Lexington: The University Press of Kentucky, 1986.

Budapest, Z. [Zsusanna]. *The Holy Book of Women's Mysteries*. Part 1. Los Angeles, CA: Susan B. Anthony Coven, 1979.

Clarson, Laura G. *Tarot Unveiled: The Method to its Magic*. Stamford, CT: U.S. Games Systems, 1988.

Clinton, Hilary Rodham. *It Takes a Village*. New York: Simon & Schuster, 1996.

Echols, Signe E., Robert Mueller, and Sandra A. Thomson. *Spiritual Tarot*. New York: Avon, 1996.

Elbow, Peter. *Writing with Power*. New York: Oxford UP, 1981.

Estes, Clarissa Pinkola. *Women Who Run with the Wolves: Myths and Stories of the Wild Woman Archetype*. New York: Ballantine, 1992.

Fairfield, Gail. *Choice Centered Tarot*. Smithville, IN: Ramp Creek, 1984.

Fowler, W. Warde. *Religious Experience of the Roman People*. London: MacMillan, 1933.

Gendlin, Eugene T. *Focusing*. Toronto: Bantam, 1978.

Gettings, Fred. *The Book of Tarot*. London: Triune, 1973.

Gray, Eden. *The Tarot Revealed*. New York: Bell, 1969.

Greer, Mary K. *Tarot Constellations: Patterns of Personal Destiny*. North Hollywood: Newcastle, 1987.

————. *Tarot for Yourself: A Workbook for Personal Transformation*. North Hollywood: Newcastle, 1984.

Hay, Louise. *You Can Heal Your Life*. Carson, CA: Hay House. 1984

Hemingway, Ernest. *For Whom the Bell Tolls*. New York: Scribner's. 1940.

Henry, Thomas R. "The Smithsonian Institution." *The National Geographic Magazine*. September 1948. pp. 325–48.

Hollander, P. Scott. *Tarot for Beginners*. St. Paul, MN: Llewellyn, 1996.

James, Muriel, and Dorothy Jongeward. *Born to Win: Transactional Analysis with Gestalt Experiments*. New York: Signet, 1978 (1971).

Johnson, Cait. *Tarot for Everyday*. Wappingers Falls, NY: Shawangunk, 1994.

Kaplan, Stuart. *Tarot Classic*. New York: Grosset & Dunlap, 1972.

Kabat-Zinn, Jon. *Wherever You Go, There You Are*. New York: Hyperion, 1994

Kipling, Rudyard. "If." *Kipling: A Selection of His Stories and Poems*. Vol. II. John Beecroft, ed. Garden City, NY: Doubleday, n.d.

Lindbergh, Anne Morrow. *Gift from the Sea*. New York: Pantheon, 1955.

Matthews, Caitlin. *Sophia: Goddess of Wisdom*. London: Aquarian, 1991.

Monaghan, Patricia. *The Book of Goddesses and Heroines*. St. Paul, MN: Llewellyn, 1990.

Moore, Robert, and Douglas Gillette. *King/Warrior/Magician/Lover: Rediscovering the Archetypes of the Mature Masculine*. New York: Harper Collins, 1990.

Moore, Thomas. *Care of the Soul*. New York: Harper-Collins, 1992.

Mountainwater, Shekinah. *Ariadne's Thread: A Workbook of Goddess Magic*. Freedom, CA: The Crossing Press, 1991.

Murray, Alexander S. *Who's Who in Mythology*. New York: Wings, 1988.

Nichols, Sallie. *Jung and the Tarot*. York Beach, ME: Weiser, 1980.

Noble, Vicki, and Jonathan Tenney. *The Motherpeace Tarot Playbook*. Berkeley, CA: Wingbow, 1986.

Plutarch, "Moralia," cited by Miriam Robbins Dexter. *Whence the Goddesses: A Source Book*. New York: Pergamon, 1990.

Ray, John. *English Proverbs*. cited in *The Home Book of Quotations Classical and Modern*. Burton Stevenson, ed. New York: Dodd, Mead, & Co., 1934.

Rilke, Rainer Maria. *Letters to a Young Poet*. M.D. Herter Norton, trans. New York: Norton, 1934.

———. *Selected Poems of Rainer Maria Rilke*. Robert Bly, trans. New York: Harper & Row, 1981.

Roberts, Elizabeth, and Elias Amidon. *Earth Prayers*. San Francisco: Harper, 1991.

Sinetar, Marsha. *Do What You Love, The Money Will Follow: Discovering Your Right Livelihood*. New York: Dell, 1990.

Stevenson, Burton, ed. *The Macmillan Book of Proverbs, Maxims and Famous Phrases*. New York: Macmillan, 1948.

Sun Tzu. *The Art of War*. Thomas Cleary, trans. Boston: Shambhala, 1988.

Waite, Arthur Edward. *The Pictorial Key to the Tarot*. Blauvelt, NY: Rudolf Steiner Publications, 1971.

Walker, Barbara. *Secrets of the Tarot*. San Francisco: Harper, 1984.

———. *The Woman's Ecyclopedia of Myths and Secrets*. San Francisco: Harper, 1983.

Whitman, Walt. "Song of the Open Road." *Leaves of Grass, Book VII*. 1891–2. New York: Modern Library.

———. "A Song of the Rolling Earth." *Leaves of Grass, Book XVI*. 1891–2. New York: Modern Library.

THE SACRED CIRCLE TAROT
A Celtic Pagan Journey
Anna Franklin, Illustrated by Paul Mason

The *Sacred Circle Tarot* is a new concept in tarot design, combining photographs, computer imaging, and traditional drawing techniques to create stunning images. It draws on the Pagan heritage of Britain and Ireland, its sacred sites and landscapes. Key symbols unlock the deepest levels of Pagan teaching.

The imagery of the cards is designed to work on a number of levels, serving as a tool not only for divination but to facilitate meditation, personal growth and spiritual development. The "sacred circle" refers to the progress of the initiate from undirected energy, through dawning consciousness, to the death of the old self and the emergence of the new.

The major arcana is modified somewhat to fit the pagan theme of the deck. For example, "The Fool" becomes "The Green Man," "The Heirophant" becomes "The Druid," and "The World" becomes "The World Tree." The accompanying book gives a full explanation of the symbolism in the cards and their divinatory meanings.

1-56718-457-X, Boxed Kit: 78 full-color cards; 288 pp., 6 x 9 book . **$29.95**

THE CELTIC DRAGON TAROT
D. J. Conway and Lisa Hunt

Are dragons real? Since they do not live on the physical plane, scientists cannot trap and dissect them. Yet magicians and psychics who have explored the astral realms know firsthand that dragons do indeed exist, and that they make very powerful comagicians. Dragons tap into deeper currents of elemental energies than humans. Because of their ancient wisdom, dragons are valuable contacts to call upon when performing any type of divination, such as the laying out of tarot cards. Tarot decks and other divination tools seem to fascinate them. *The Celtic Dragon Tarot* is the first deck to use the potent energies of dragons for divination, magickal spell working, and meditation.

Ancient mapmakers noted every unknown territory with the phrase "Here be dragons." Both tarot and magick have many uncharted areas. Not only will you discover dragons waiting there, but you will also find them to be extremely helpful when you give them the chance.

1-56718-182-1, Boxed Kit: 78 full-color cards; 216 pp., 6 x 9 book **$29.95**

SHAPESHIFTER TAROT
D. J. Conway and Sirona Knight
Illustrated by Lisa Hunt

Like the ancient Celts, you can now practice the shamanic art of shapeshifting and access the knowledge of the eagle, the oak tree or the ocean: wisdom that is inherently yours and resides within your very being. *The Shapeshifter Tarot* kit is your bridge between humans, animals and nature. The cards in this deck act as merging tools, allowing you to tap into the many different animal energies, together with the elemental qualities of air, fire, water and earth.

The accompanying book gives detailed explanations on how to use the cards, along with their full esoteric meanings, and mythological and magical roots. Exercises in shapeshifting, moving through gateways, doubling out, meditation and guided imagery give you the opportunity to enhance your levels of perception and awareness, allowing you to hone and accentuate your magical understanding and skill.

1-56718-384-0, Boxed Kit: 81 full-color cards, instruction book $29.95

LEGEND
The Arthurian Tarot
Anna-Marie Ferguson

Gallery artist and writer Anna-Marie Ferguson paires the ancient divinatory system of the tarot with the Arthurian myth to create *Legend: The Arthurian Tarot*. The exquisitely beautiful watercolor paintings of this tarot deck illustrate characters, places, and tales from the legends that blend traditional tarot symbolism with the Pagan and Christian symbolism.

Each card represents the Arthurian counterpart to tarot's traditional figures, such as Merlin as the Magician, Morgan le Fay as the Moon, Mordred as the King of Swords, and Arthur as the Emperor. Accompanying the deck is a decorative layout sheet in the format of the Celtic Cross to inspire and guide your readings, as well as the book *Keeper of Words,* which lists the divinatory meanings of the cards, the cards' symbolism, and the telling of the legend associated with each card. This visionary tarot encompasses all the complex situations life has to offer—trials, challenges, and rewards—to help you cultivate a close awareness of your past, present, and future through the richness of the Arthurian legend . . . a legend which continues to court the imagination and speak to the souls of people everywhere.

1-56718-267-4, Boxed Kit: Deck: 78 full-color cards;
Layout sheet: 21 x 24, four-color; 272 pp., 6 x 9 book, illus., $34.95

TO ORDER, CALL 1-800-THE MOON
Prices subject to change without notice

THE WITCHES TAROT KIT
Ellen Cannon Reed, illustrated by Martin Cannon

Previously sold separately, *The Witches Tarot* book and deck are now packaged together as a complete kit, just in time for the holiday season.

This tarot deck has become a favorite among paganfolk who enjoy the presentation of the mystical Qabalistic symbolism from a clear and distinctly Pagan point of view. Creator Ellen Cannon Reed has replaced the traditional Devil with The Horned One, the Hierophant with the High Priest, and the Hermit with the Seeker. Each of the Magical Spheres is included, in striking color, on the corresponding cards. Even nonpagans have reported excellent results with the cards and appreciate their colorful and timeless beauty.

In the book, Reed defines the complex, inner workings of the Qabala. She includes is a complete section on divination, with several layout patterns. In addition, she provides instruction on using the cards for Pathworking, or astral journeys through the Tree of Life. An appendix gives a list of correspondences for each of the Paths including the associated Tarot card, Hebrew letter, colors, astrological attribution, animal, gem, and suggested meditation.

1-56718-558-4, Boxed Kit: Deck: 78 full-color cards; Layout sheet: 21 x 24
320 pp., 5.25 x 8 book   **$34.95**

GOLDEN DAWN MAGICAL TAROT
Sandra Tabatha Cicero
Formerly titled
The New Golden Dawn Ritual Tarot Deck

Encouraged by famed occultist Israel Regardie himself, this tarot deck is a visually stunning, sensual deck that skillfully blends the descriptions given in Golden Dawn initiation ceremonies with traditional tarot imagery.

From its inception 100 years ago, the Hermetic Order of the Golden Dawn continues to be the authority on the initiatory and meditative teachings of the Tarot. The Golden Dawn used certain cards in its initiation rituals. Now a deck incorporates all of the temple symbolism needed for use in the Golden Dawn rituals.

Meditation on the Major Arcana cards can lead to a lightning flash of enlightenment and help you on your spiritual path. It is for anyone who wants a reliable Tarot deck that follows the Western magickal tradition.

1-56718-125-2, Boxed Kit: 79-card deck and 160-pp. booklet   **$19.95**

TO ORDER, CALL 1-800-THE MOON
Prices subject to change without notice